RETREAT DYNAMICS

RETREAT DYNAMICS

Joseph B. Simons, C.S.C.

FIDES PUBLISHERS, INC.   NOTRE DAME, IND.

preface

In facing the uncertain future of religious exploration, it becomes more and more clear that psychological techniques and insights must be sincerely examined in an effort to understand much of what we are attempting to accomplish. We know from past experience that far too often the psychological has been mistaken for the religious to the detriment of both. If we are to escape this kind of potential harm in the future, it is important for us to be comfortable in both areas of inquiry.

The day of extreme fear and defensiveness in the face of the psychological has disappeared from the Church, but there are those still uncomfortable concerning the methods and discoveries of psychology. Because of this, it is expected that many will have difficulty with the contents of this volume. In order that there be no misunderstanding, it should be stated at the outset that serious attempts were made to avoid any unnecessary concern along these lines. On the contrary, the primary effort was to demonstrate the ease with which religion may move in the atmosphere provided by psychology and be enhanced by its ventilation.

In attempting to recall the number of persons who have helped make this book a reality, I have been amazed at the size of the debt owed. From those who shared their misgivings or encouragement to the retreatants who demonstrated almost infinite patience with my imperfect attempts, I drew the courage and strength necessary for the task. It would be impossible to begin to mention the number of persons who have been involved in the effort, but it would be a serious breach of justice not to mention Mrs. Miriam Lorch whose advice and aid extended to every page of the manuscript. The many who cannot be mentioned by name know their place in the effort and my thanks for their involvement.

Joseph B. Simons

Notre Dame, Indiana
April, 1967

CONTENTS

I. the controversy

In recent issues of the journal, *Review for Religious,* a controversy has developed concerning the proper format for retreats, especially the annual retreat for religious. Whether the individual author favors adopting a new format to enrich the retreat experience or insists that changing the basic form would render the classical method ineffective as a means of sanctification, there seems to be little doubt in my mind that the retreat method and structure are being critically reexamined. This point can be illustrated further by the consistent stand taken by three authors who otherwise find themselves divided as to the most beneficial retreat format.

> We need not be surprised, therefore that the annual retreat for religious has also become the object of critical analysis. Much healthy discussion has taken place both as to the content of retreats as well as to the method of conducting them.[1]

> As in so many other areas of the Church today, so in the matter of retreats there is much reinvestigation and change. Retreats take many different forms these days. The topic of adaptation in the presentation of retreats to youth seems to be foremost in the discussions among retreat directors.[2]

> The winds of change are blowing open many doors. One of these is the long-closed door of community retreats. For the past few years there have been a number of attempts to analyze the matter and methods of retreats, discussing the findings of surveys taken, as well as suggestions for alterations. In general, there seems to be a growing sense of dissatisfaction with the very structure of retreats, and the purpose of this article is to open up the subject for wider discussion.[3]

An atmosphere conducive to questioning is growing within the Church which has already resulted in a great deal of change. It is hardly surprising that the retreat as a form of sanctification is being reexamined to discover whether or not it has lost some of its fundamental meaning during the many years since it was first introduced into the Church. In an age that has seen such radical changes in the liturgy of the Mass, surely only the most rigid would refuse to examine the retreat for potential changes which might prove efficacious in the plan of salvation.

In order to give some insight into the dimensions of the controversy, the substance of two articles will be considered which are fundamentally opposed to one another in their vision of the most efficacious form for future retreats. In a very stimulating article, Father Andrew Auw, ponders openly whether the communal nature of retreats might be emphasized more in order to keep in closer touch with the spirit of a post-conciliar age. Father Ambrose de Groot reacts against this kind of thinking by suggesting that to so alter the retreat format would be to destroy not only a valuable but even a necessary means of sanctification for religious so constantly caught up in the activity of a modern world.

In introducing a communal dimension into the retreat format, there is normally a rejection of any terminology suggesting escape from the world as the goal of such retreats. It is felt that many, by emphasizing the isolation from the world, have introduced a note of the unreal into any thoughts, meditations, or inspirations which normally occur during the period set aside for reflection away from the intensity of daily activities. To suggest that the degree of isolation necessarily implies a more profoundly spiritual experience strikes many as not only simplistic but as fundamentally false.

Writers such as Father Auw are rather looking for a new dimension to the personal encounter with Christ which is the goal of the retreat for all Christians. While seeking the most profound depths of such an encounter, they are not satisfied that increasing the degree of silence or the intensity of the spiritual exercises will result necessarily in probing further into the spiritual realm of any individual. Individuals are rather looking at radical new forms to aid the retreatant in exploring a dimension which they feel has been slighted due to an over-emphasis on individual spirituality.

In an attempt to return to the spirit of apostolic times, such authors hope to establish within the context of the retreat an emphasis on the discovery of Christ's love within the context of community. Though retreats are almost always given to groups of people, the communal aspect of such experiences has been deemphasized to the point of extinction. The conferences, the readings, and the silence of the retreat tend to all but extinguish the sense of community which can and should be a part of any religious experience which is genuine.

For a truly balanced approach to spirituality, our experience must effectively fuse the individual and communal nature of Christianity. It is difficult indeed to arrive at a genuine insight into Christ's revelation when forced by circumstances into an introspection which tends to remove the ideas, reflections, and even presence of others.

Without eliminating the opportunity for personal reflection in a retreat, periods of common reflection and discussion should be introduced. An insight shared with a group can easily be discovered to lack a great deal when checked against the intelligence and common resources normally present within any given group of people. On a more fundamental level, to share a personal experience which drew one closer to the love of Christ gives to others the opportunity to realize something of that same love and deepen their own spirituality. As an integral part of the retreat format, such communal sharing of experiences would appear to be fundamentally sound in that it would tend to increase the awareness of Christ's presence among those engaged in such sharing.

> We have come to understand a retreat as an opportunity to come away from one type of Christ-encounter in order to experience another type of Christ-encounter in the reflective atmosphere of a quiet place. Like the early Apostles, we put

aside not only our nets and our boats but even our teaching and preaching in order to renew the spirit of Christ within us.

There is one great difference, however, in the analogy with the Apostles; and it lies in the fact that unlike us, the Apostles went on retreat *as a community*. They were able to experience the love of Christ not merely as individuals but also as a community. After each retreat they returned more united as Christians, growing in love until they attained the post-Pentecost oneness of heart described in the book of Acts.[4]

Many who desire communal experience as part of the retreat format maintain that the present mode is too individualistic in its means. Any occasion that would bring love to the community as the result of such an experience would have to be drawn from a personal renewal which would individually draw one closer to the love of Christ. In its attempt to attain this goal, there has been no doubt that the traditional retreat has been effective. The desire is not to condemn the retreat as we have all known it; but rather to look to new methods which will bring persons to dimensions thus far overlooked in terms of goals for the retreat experience.

In emphasizing the social nature of the Church in a post-conciliar age, many point to such documents as Pope Paul's encyclical *Ecclesiam Suam*, the *Constitution on the Liturgy* and the *Constitution on the Church* which have an awareness of the Church's social nature and mission as their main thrust. In reading these documents, one is made aware again and again of the social dimensions of our salvation and sanctification. To fail to see this renewed emphasis on communal awareness within the context of the Church's mission is to miss one of the basic touchstones upon which renewal is erected.

From these documents as well as the atmosphere which surrounds the spirit of Christian renewal within the Church today, one is constantly reminded of the social dimension which his personal commitment to Christ must encompass. The love of Christ can only result in sterility unless it encompasses an awareness, concern, and commitment to the total Christ as concretized in the human beings with whom he comes in contact. Without a rich and deep concern for his brothers who are suffering disease and discrimination, who are enduring poverty and despair, who are fighting to retain even a spark of the human dignity that is their right, the Christian is nominal only by reason of his life's witness.

If the end sought by our Christian commitment is so clearly recognized as being fundamentally social in nature, can we fail to introduce communal notions into our traditional means toward that end? Any attempt to renew and revitalize our Christian life should use means which are appropriate to the goal in view. It follows that if we fail to share with others the experiences which have drawn them closer to Christ it might make the retreat experience less enriching than it would otherwise be. Since sharing ideas, reflections, and concerns reveals a new depth to common experiences, it is shortsighted to unnecessarily neglect to incorporate such experiences into the retreat format.

From an examination of scripture, it becomes obvious that our Christian goal is to encounter Christ in the richest, deepest, and most profound manner available to us. Though the term encounter has been abused during recent years, this can be no excuse for us not to realize that encounter with Christ in the genuine sense of that word is and will remain a basic goal of our life. To defend ourselves against the struggle implied in the experience of Christian encounter by scoffing at the degree to which the term is overused is to attempt an escape from a life project we know must be ours regardless of the temper or emphasis of any given age.

Whether we read the documents of the Church or return to the wellspring of scripture, it is obvious that both Christ and the Church remind us that we encounter Christ when we encounter other human beings. Christ has told us that our salvation will depend upon our love for others when they were hungry, thirsty, naked, or imprisoned. Such love, concern and compassion for men who surround us in our daily lives is love for Christ.

From a relatively superficial examination of human experience, it becomes clear that the difficulties implicit in attempting to encounter another without his presence are enormous. One might have some sense of the despair the destitute individual suffers when trapped in the torture of slum living by reading about the problem, but surely this cannot compare to actually living with such a desperate man, hearing him speak, experiencing his emotions, and feeling his fear. Though it is impossible to completely share the experiences of another human being, his presence removes so many obvious obstacles to such union.

The goal of introducing methods into the retreat experience which would allow intimacy between the community assembled is an attempt to introduce a new dimension into the retreat experience. With the obvious need in the world for the genuine sense of community, each individual Christian must take every opportunity to expand his understanding of the bonds which draw community members together. In order to be able to share the sense of community with those who have not had the advantage of such an experience, it is obvious that the one attempting to share must participate in the richest form of communal life available. The one who is involved in the richest form of community life is not only able to gain insight into the meaning of such an experience for himself; but also inspired to bring it to others.

The prime requisite for encounter is presence, a presence which makes a person completely open to the needs of another. This may explain why so many retreatants in the past have failed to encounter Christ on retreat. It may explain why, year after year, religious come away from their retreat feeling as if "nothing happened."

Encountering Christ is very difficult because we must actually experience the presence of a person in order to effect this unique relationship. In a way we are like the apostles after the ascension. Christ, the historical person they knew and loved, was gone. They could not see his face nor hear his voice nor feel his touch. He simply was not present to them as before, and it seemed as if they would never be able to encounter him again on this earth.

Then a marvelous thing happened. As Christ had instructed them to do, they gathered about a table and, together, they renewed the memorial of his passion and they rediscovered Christ. In breaking bread together, they experienced the person of Christ in the Christ-person next to them. It was a new encounter, but an authentic one. The apostles not only encountered Christ in community, *but as community*.

There is every reason to believe that a similar experience can be ours to share on retreat.[5]

In order to bring the controversy into sharper focus, it would be relevant and helpful to reflect on the thoughts of Father Ambrose de Groot in his article published by *Review for Religious*. In fairness to the opinions expressed, it should be noted that the outlook suggested by the article is shared by many who have reflected seriously on the question at hand. Further substantiating their position is the fact that great numbers of those questioning a new retreat format, like Father De Groot, have had many years of experience in retreat work and have been impressed by the significance of the classical method.

In order to properly understand the position taken, one must be willing to admit that many mistakes have been made by individuals and religious communities in their efforts to adapt to the spirit of renewal. In an age when many guidelines of the past have been eliminated, there has been a tendency to accept change as an end in itself. Some have lost sight of the more fundamental meaning embodied in the Christian doctrine by mistaking the novelty of change as the end in view for renewal.

The temper of individuals and a misunderstanding of the mind of the Church have already done much harm to religious discipline in some communities.[6]

It is not surprising that many look with a great deal of suspicion upon any attempt to alter the form of the retreat which has proven so valuable over the centuries as a source of grace and inspiration. If the retreat were to lose any of its meaning because some felt "it was time" to change, there is reason to do everything possible to oppose such a movement. There need be no apology for questioning the value of change in a means of sanctification which has proved itself over the centuries.

The traditional form of retreat has always meant removing oneself from the cares, troubles, struggles, and intensity of daily existence into a place of silence, reflection and solitude for a period of time. This escape from the pressures of "normal" life has had as its goal the discovery of Christ's presence and love in a richer and more meaningful way. Experience has shown us that such periods of withdrawal make it more possible to live closely to Christ and his love. In the atmosphere which surrounds the retreat, much truth concerning the individual and his spirituality unfolds which ultimately enriches the life to which one must return after the retreat has ended.

To ask the justification for introducing such things as group discussions into an otherwise reflective and silent period does not seem to be unreasonable. If the retreatant has gone to a great amount of effort to attain the solitude of the retreat, can there be a rationale for introducing things which would disrupt that solitude? It is from a reasonable basis that many are questioning the new retreat format they see emerging.

Another fear expressed on the part of many springs from the amount of "new theology" which has become so much a part of the modern retreat. If the retreat becomes dominated by new concepts in theology, many feel there is real danger that the foundations upon which our Christian life is based will be diluted or lost. In the retreat format which has been so much a part of our lives until recent years, it was the basic tenets of Christianity which formed the core of emphasis. The very concerns, anxieties, and distress of life which caused the individual to feel the need of the solitude and reflective atmosphere of a retreat were discovered to be the things which obscured the more fundamental truths of Christianity.

In reacting against the suggestion that the community discover itself during the annual retreat, many question the involvement of religious community members during the year.

The religious who truly lives according to the norms of community life certainly can be in no real need for special dialogue during the occasion of a retreat. To suggest that community members dialogue during the time set aside for special reflection on the love of Christ would appear to be overlooking the fact that there are numerous occasions for such dialogue during the year. It would seem those suggesting the introduction of dialogue into retreat are the ones guilty of selfish and self-centered attitudes which negate the possibility of the sense of community they are requesting.

> By encountering Christ present in the person of each other as a community they (the apostles) encountered Christ himself. This is all very beautiful and, no doubt, very true. But are not we religious doing this all year round? Have we so lost sight of the spiritual advantages which are part of the very structure of our communal life that they no longer have any meaning for us?[7]

The quotation poses some rather fundamental questions. We must question whether or not we are actively engaged in witnessing the value of community in the world. For a world so desperately in need of the sense of community, the life of the religious in genuine community becomes even more necessary if the good news of the gospel is to be preached in its fullness. In view of the alienation which surrounds modern industrial society, the religious must make special effort to probe honestly within himself to ask whether or not he is honest in his efforts to effect a true sense of community within his own congregation.

> It is very difficult for me to comprehend the enthusiasm which is displayed at times by those who have made such a community retreat, for instance, the Better World Retreat. They seem so fascinated by the wonderful experience of having lived together for a week in a real Christian community; how they prayed together; offered the Holy Sacrifice together; discussed the spiritual life and its problems together; how they loved one another in true fraternal charity. One cannot help but wonder where they have been all their religious lives. . . . Can a religious become such a robot in an

atmosphere which was especially designed by his founder and the Church herself to be one of community prayer, worship, love and dialogue? Can he allow familiarity to breed such an apathy that he becomes impervious to the glorious opportunities communal life offers to live his Christian consecration all year round as perfectly as any of the early Christians?[8]

It is not surprising that many find themselves questioning the sincerity of attempts to introduce dialogue into the retreat format. One who did not wonder whether the desire for communication during the period of retreat was not just an attempt to escape the difficulties encountered in the demands silence imposes on the individual, would certainly be questioned by the honest observer. If anyone were to honestly recall the kind of demands God has imposed when he stands alone before him, it is not unreasonable to suggest to that same person that there may lie within him a desire to escape such a burden. To reflect on the work involved in attaining a personal sense of God's presence making genuine prayer possible at its most significant level is to recall a task not easily undertaken save by the most generous. The activity of the dialogue could be an easy release from the work and burdens implicit in the solitude which may reveal the love of Christ at its most significant depths.

If by their attempts to introduce dialogue into the retreat format some are attempting to escape the depths of experience the retreat is intended to explore, there is no doubt that such attempts are doomed from the start. Any change in the means suggested for our increased spirituality must deepen the experience of grace or be immediately discarded as not only worthless but also dangerous. The burden of proof must also remain on the shoulders of those who suggest the change in any means or method which has survived the ebb and tide of many modern but ineffective attempts at adaptation.

If dialogue were to become a permanent part of the retreat format, there is real danger that the retreat could become an intellectual exercise with those engaged in the dialogue becoming fascinated by the intricacies of moral or dogmatic theology.

There is little doubt about the common experience shared by many which points to the fact that some tend to want to impress others with their knowledge and command of subject matter. When and if retreats become intellectual in nature, they will have lost their basic rationale for existence.

> We may not approach a retreat as we would a seminar or X panel discussion. We go into retreat to renew our spiritual life, to reorientate our way of thinking, to recharge our hearts with the love for Christ that burned there on the day we first pronounced our vows. The retreat is not primarily a time to nourish our minds. That obviously is part of it. But we nourish our minds and reorientate our thinking in order to move our hearts to greater love and generosity. The spiritual life is not primarily an intellectual affair — though many moderns seem to be swerving in that direction. Intellectualism is growing into a modern cult. A false emphasis is placed on theological and psychological learning as if it were on a par with sanctity itself.[9]

If the danger is that dialogue within the retreat will place this kind of false emphasis on intellectuality, then there surely can be no reason to discuss the topic further. Father De Groot points to the fact that one cannot allow the retreat to become an intellectual affair for fear of changing its fundamental nature. He is certainly pointing to a conclusion which is obvious to all. There are times and places for an emphasis on this nourishment of mind and the retreat period simply cannot be one of them.

Underlying all of the objections to introducing dialogue into the retreat appears to be the fear that the modern reaction against an individualistic spirituality has gotten out of hand. Possibly the time has already come when we must begin to look to the possibility of an extreme ecclesial spirituality. While the council has emphasized the need for more emphasis on the social concerns of the Church, it has also stressed the basic need of prayer, silence, and contemplation in order to lead the full Christian life.

It would seem valuable to now draw back from the specific and look at the general guidelines which might be suggested for the Church in a period of flux. By withdrawing from any particular controversy and focusing on general goals and means toward those goals, it is hoped that some of the emotional response might be set aside temporarily which necessarily permeates any discussion concerning a specific change within the Church's structure. An abstract consideration of the general guidelines which naturally suggest themselves should enable one to discover his present stance more accurately and direct his movement accordingly.

In order to begin any discussion of the post-conciliar Church, it is important for all to recognize and admit that the Church is experiencing a revolution. There may be some semantic difficulty with the term revolution, but there is little doubt that the Church is experiencing radical changes at all levels of her existence, including her social, political, philosophical, cultural and religious structures. Since all attempts to restructure are, to a greater or lesser degree, being opposed from within, it would not appear inappropriate to use the notion of revolution to describe the movement.

If one thing deserves emphasis in an attempt to describe the present reform movement within the Church, it is the fact that both the move to reform as well as opposition to the reform come from the actions of dedicated men operating within the framework of the Catholic Church. Drawing inspiration from the same scriptural content, the same documents of the Church, the same historical knowledge, and the same dedication to the goals of Christianity, men of good will are sharply divided on what appears to be an infinity of issues. If a moral miracle is operating within the Church today, it is the miracle of unity which has allowed such diverse opinions to exist in often bitter form without experiencing the painful schisms of the past.

It must be emphasized, however, that the present "revolution" is developing *from within* and not *against* the Church. Its proponents consider themselves Catholic, have every intention of remaining so, and are convinced that their desire for reform proceed from the Church's own spirit, not against it. What they are rebelling against is not, in their eyes, anything essential to Catholicism, but a contingent historical configuration which no longer has whatever *raison d'être* it may once have had, and now only hinders the action of the Spirit.[10]

As will be regularly emphasized by those embroiled within any given controversy concerning change, we must be constantly aware of the distinction between those forms of Church worship which are divinely inspired and those which are humanly inspired. Though there are clear examples of divinely inspired ritual, this light shines diffusely at times and leaves many at odds in describing the source of inspiration in several areas of Church rite and ritual. Mistakes will be avoided by the over-enthusiastic, but the area of doubt remaining continues to be broad and perplexing for those who are genuinely striving to discover guidelines in an age which tends to produce more questions than answers.

If one were to become so confused as to think that every area not clearly an example of divine inspiration *ipso facto* needs change, he would be missing the entire rationale for renewal in the Church. When one considers the fact that the rituals which are being so rapidly altered have been a genuine source of stability for the Church during so many ages that sought change, it gives him sound reason to pause and consider his action well before moving rapidly toward a form of renewal which may or may not result in the desired effect. The spirit of novelty appears to be the thrust of the desire for change among many who are superficially involved in the spirit of renewal. What will become of these persons when the novelty stabilizes and the new becomes old?

Many have allowed the ritual forms of the Church to become so stagnant that they have lost the meaning for their existence. When Christ instituted the Eucharist, he did not so burden the Apostles with rubrics that they lost sight of the sign value of the human symbols employed. In choosing the emotional symbol of the meal to envelop the most significant divine mystery, Christ pointed to his expectation that the emotions and the complete human response were to be a genuine part of the sacramental life of the Church. While many are severely criticized in their attempt to return the human response to the occasion of grace, there is every reason to believe that this was a genuine and significant part of Christ's request to "Do *this* in remembrance of me."

In an age when the emphasis within the Church focused on the precise rendition of rubrical form in effecting the sacraments, Catholics became too readily abstracted from themselves in the form of participation available to them. Sharing the sense of emotional presence and involvement so apparent in the early Church was looked upon with a great deal of suspicion. Christ's command of love and his expressions of love to the human persons he encountered were softened to accommodate the fearful.

If the individual did not at the same time consider the other danger implicit in the expression of emotion, he would be blinding himself to one of the most significant problems true Christians face in a period of renewal. The Christian who discovers himself divinizing the emotions and making the expression of emotional love the only goal of the Christian message must realize that he has fallen into the subtlest snare present in a post-conciliar age. In view of the sudden emphasis on the role of the emotions in the Christian life, there need be no anguish in discovering an all too human response in our attempts to worship. Rather than allow fear to block a discovery of the proper role of the emotions, each person must become more sensitive to the balance he should strike and move surely but patiently toward that equilibrium which allows a genuine exercise of emotion in the divine worship of God.

By attending exclusively either to their natural, intrinsic religious value, or to the supernatural value which they possess by reason of this divine employment, one falls into either of two typical wrong attitudes toward them. One is a false supernaturalism which is insensitive to the natural function of the sacraments and sacramentals as expressions of and helps for man's religious life. The distinctive roles of ritual, sermon and song are to a large degree lost sight of in a view that lumps them all together under the colorless concept, "means of grace."

. . . On the other hand, there is a religious humanism which so fixes its attention on natural religious values that it is insufficiently mindful of the supernatural function of all religious activity in the Christian economy. It tends to see religion in the pattern of a work of art. It labors to make the liturgy of the Church more beautiful, its preaching more eloquent, its government more efficient. But it forgets that, far more important than the intrinsic perfection of these human constructions is the merciful intervention of God, who vouchsafes to employ these "unprofitable servants" in extending to man a communion with himself that utterly transcends the value and efficacy of the intermediaries.[11]

If fear is engendered in the Christian person as a result of his emotional involvement and he begins to guard himself from such fear, there is a real danger that he will begin to lose consciousness of himself and substitute for this awareness of self an attempt to play the role of the "ideal Christian" at prayer. We all too easily lose sight of ourselves and begin to speak to Christ as if we were on a stage and performing a role, and are then obviously no longer capable of giving Christ the genuine gift of self he so clearly requests.

The sense of peace and calm that appears when one is most conscious of himself is most important in a true expression of worship. Such an underlying peace appears even at the time one is considering the greatest periods of anguish, frustration, and despair present in working out salvation. This should not be surprising in view of the recurring theme of peace which occurs throughout the entire New Testament message. Though Christ never promised that our lot would be pleasant, he did promise us peace. When that peace comes, it is the result of being aware of oneself whether that self-awareness involves joy or sadness, love or hate, calm or frustration. Christ asked for the gift of self. Can we possibly give him anything less?

If there has been an overemphasis on the Church's lack of emotionality in worship, it is because the Church has been a

sign to the world of the lack of emotion that all institutions
and individuals have experienced in their daily concerns. The
Church's attempt to introduce clear and meaningful guidelines
for worship manifested to non-Catholics around the world a
sense of the magical. In their attempts to understand the ritual
and rite of the Church, non-Catholics were constantly speaking
in terms which would suggest superstition.

The fact is that the entire world is just beginning to become
conscious of the proper role of the emotions. Not until the work
of Freud began to make us conscious of the emotional world
in which we are enveloped did the world become seriously
concerned with the total human response. Can it be any wonder
that we are just now becoming genuinely concerned with the
role of emotion in worship?

In exploring the emotional experience possible during the
time of retreat, the feeling is that an entirely new dimension may
be introduced into an already effective source of grace. By
exploring the emotional depth of an individual's spirituality,
it is personally felt that not only will a new dimension be discovered; but the retreat will become something much richer,
deeper, and more meaningful than ever previously experienced.

The sense of community within the context of retreat may
be tapped in genuine ways which have been previously ignored.
Although many will continue to suspect such desire for community love is nothing more than an escape from the rigors of
silence, personal experience leads many to believe the opposite.
Under the pressure of daily concerns, fears, and anxieties, true
communication between even the most intimate members of
a strong religious community loses much of the ideal we sense
in reading the Acts of the Apostles. Petty grievances can readily
build over the course of time into what appears to be in-
surmountable blocks to communication, to say nothing of friendship. If the occasion of the retreat is not the ideal time for
exploring together these attitudes which are fundamentally
unchristian in nature, then there would appear to be some
reason to request that we reconsider those same goals.

We might suggest that even the most intimate friendships

be examined under the light of community involvement. Though the individuals may be unaware of negative effects resulting from a genuine friendship, the rest of the community may consider the friendship exclusive or false in ways which could reveal a depth fundamentally more Christian in its outlook or effect. If the friendship is rather an ideal of some kind for others, what could be more generous than sharing with others the nature and trials of its bond. If we are to do anything with our life as true Christians, it is to explore the dimensions of love within ourselves and others.

Only by really sensing the true nature of Christian love in all its dimensions, may we hope to bring such love to others. When one speaks of "teaching" others to love, a certain sense of the unreal springs from within the lover. Unless one witnesses love by his presence, his desire to bring love to others may wither and die for lack of emotional nourishment. The time of retreat is the time to experience love between the members of the Christian community assembled or the meaning of the retreat experience is lost for those who would witness by their presence more than their words.

If the suggestion that people assembled for a retreat might discuss the dimensions of their religious experience together disturbs some, one wonders about the source of such disturbance. Once the individual has felt the power of an honest statement by a fellow Christian revealing his relationship to Christ, there is little doubt concerning the personal value of such an experience. Further, there no longer is any doubt that the need for conversion might spring from a sluggish mentality which would turn to discussion in order to escape the pressure of silence.

If one experiences retreat in the face of an honest discussion of an individual's personal relationship with Christ, it might be the escape from pondering the strength of his own similar relationship. When fear becomes manifest on such an occasion, it is most likely to be the fear that my own experience is not as relevant as that just expressed. The thought that one might never have really been aware of his own relationship to Christ with sufficient clarity to articulate it meaningfully to himself or others would be even more disturbing.

For many who have allowed themselves to delve honestly into discussions with meaningful goals, a fear exists that such discussion may reveal to them a complete lack of religious commitment. There is no hope to ever descend beneath the veneer of ritualism and really discover the depths of Christ's love. If such a fear holds sway when one is able to transcend this fear and risk himself in the presence of others, only then will he find himself in relation to Christ and have a foundation upon which to build a dynamic and growing spirituality. The starting point may not be that preconceived in formulating one's ideal concept of his relationship to Christ, but it will be genuinely a manifestation of himself and reflect the kind of reality which can grow in the nourishment of others.

While such discovery is certainly possible within the context of retreats we have experienced for centuries, modern psychology has pointed to the unnecessary burden placed on the individual hoping to discover himself without the presence and help of others. If the self which we are discovering is genuinely Christian in nature, why should we resist the aids which have been discovered for helping us uncover this sense of self? If we really hope to find our true self and we do not fear whether or not this self is fundamentally Christian, there would seem to be no reason to resist means to this end revealed by modern psychology.

The cry against the use of psychology rings out on every side, but there is a certain hollowness in its tone. If we really rejected the use of psychology only because its basic tenets do not make mention of the religious nature of man, why would the application of its truth become rejected so completely? One comes to suspect that the rejection of psychology comes from a fear of self rather than a fear of psychology. When one honestly probes into his true identity, it will not be the use of psychological truth that presents him with doubts concerning God's existence but rather a personal lack of faith. The use of psychology reveals man at a more fundamental depth than he experienced before, and it will be in that revelation that man will also discover a depth of spirituality previously unrevealed.

This book makes no pretense about its goal. There will be no attempt to hide the fact that the intent is to persuade others of the value implicit in the use of modern knowledge to produce the religious experience at a depth as profound as possible. Experience has convinced the author that the use of group dynamics in retreat work is extremely effective in helping the retreatants to discover the workings of the Holy Spirit manifest on the retreat occasion. The book is an unabashed attempt to persuade others that such is true.

REFERENCES

1. Ambrose de Groot, O.F.M. CAP., "Retreat: Dialogue or Silence?" *Review for Religious*, v. 25 (1966), p. 828.
2. George A. Aschenbrenner, S.J., "Retreat or Community Experience," *Review for Religious*, v. 25 (1966), p. 860.
3. Andre Auw, C.P., "Community Retreats: Same Song, New Lyrics," *Review for Religious*, v. 24 (1965), p. 797.
4. Andre Auw, p. 797-8.
5. Auw, p. 799.
6. De Groot, p. 828.
7. De Groot, p. 831.
8. De Groot, p. 831.
9. De Groot, p. 833.
10. Edward D. O'Connor, C.S.C., "Revolution within the Church?" *Thought*, v. 39 (1964), p. 223.
11. O'Connor, p. 225-6.

2. philosophical foundations

In the Church today many questions are being implicitly and explicitly asked which strike at the heart of man's religious conviction. Foundations upon which it was presumed that Catholics must stand if they are to accept the doctrines of Christianity are suddenly being questioned without any apparent attempt to escape the light of Catholic dogma. Because this atmosphere of questioning prevails within the Church, the individual Catholic needs a great deal of insight to know his own attitude toward his faith, to say nothing of the courage necessary to articulate this standpoint to others.

It is much easier to discuss the changes in the liturgy, the birth control issue, or the authority of the bishop than it is to attempt to discuss the reasons underlying a particular attitude toward these questions. If an attitude toward a question has roots which are emotional, however, the discussion can become more heated than the facts of the discussion would apparently warrant. A young couple discussing the birth control issue can be expected to become emotionally involved in the discussion. But when priests discuss the issue of whether or not group dynamics might become a part of the retreat format, we do not expect the kind of passion expressed by Father De Groot in the article discussed in the first chapter.

The passion evident in many discussions of the value of retreat dynamics suggests an emotional underpinning to the discussion which does not appear on the surface. It seems to involve an attitude toward religious truth as well as a basic philosophy of man.

In the field of education, philosophical considerations clearly affect one's attitude concerning the success or failure of the present system. Philosophical analyses of the present educational system appear periodically giving fresh insight into the evolution through which education is constantly moving. By attempting a similar analysis, we can be in a better position to adequately consider the philosophical and theological justification of our position on the potential value of group dynamics.

Until recent years, the Church has almost exclusively focused on the essential nature of man in her dogmatic and moral statements. In an endeavor to discover those characteristics which are common to all men, the Church has tended to lose sight of the individuality of the person. When the existential movement attempted to stimulate men to become more conscious of their tendency to prejudge actions against an "objective" standpoint, the Church did not hesitate to condemn the movement.

A Christian existential movement has been growing within the Church despite such ecclesiastical condemnations. Those within the movement are suggesting that Christ's life was existential at its roots. By teaching the law of love to fulfill the law of the prophets, Christ, like the existentialist, was introducing the genuine value of judging by subjective, rather than by objective standards. The Christian existential movement does not accept man as pure existence any more than it does as pure essence, but there is a strong reaction against the past which has not arrived at a legitimate balance between the two views of man.

The existentialist sees man as more than his essential nature. He emphasizes the notion of man as condition. Each man is uniquely distinguished from every other man insofar as he exists interiorly and exteriorly in a particular situation. To suggest that the interior conditions of suffering, dread, and anguish or the exterior conditions of poverty, culture, and heritage do not affect man directly and mark him differently from every other man is to be blind to the reality of life.

The person who sees his own happiness achieved by conforming to some external set of norms has apparently lost contact with his own experience. Far from suggesting that there is no common nature within man, the existentialist declares that such a nature is discovered by each individual in a unique and personal manner. One need only reflect momentarily on his own experience to discover that a process which forces one to conform externally to a given standard will ultimately cause him to lose contact with himself. Thus, Christ's insistence on the virtues of compassion, love, and understanding, in the mind of the existentialist, ranks above the conformity to external norms. This was Christ's unique contribution to the Jewish law. In order for man to genuinely grow in virtue, he must practice the virtues which put him in contact with himself and promote positive attitudes toward fellow men. The function of the law is normative or that by which one may measure the extent of growth. The individual who reverses the process and "assures" himself of salvation by rigidly adhering to external standards would be missing the entire message Christ came to proclaim.

In every age of history, there have been concerted efforts by men to gain more freedom for themselves. Much time, energy, and effort have been spent by men in an effort to gain more freedom. But freedom brings with it a responsibility for action which man naturally tends to fear. The movement toward free actions is necessarily, therefore, complex at the emotional level.

By genuinely facing up to his real potential for freedom, man must also consider the proportionate responsibility he assumes when he performs a free action. A man who acts in any given manner as a result of a personal conviction which has developed within himself knows he must also hold himself responsible for any errors or injury to others which will result as a consequence of his free choice. While certain kinds of behavioral freedom may not internally affect him, genuine freedom will be a part of man and ultimately influence his life.

Though it may be for such worthy reasons as dedication to one's job or family, the fact is that most individuals create their own shackles. If I can convince myself that I must behave in a certain manner because of the demands of my work, then I have created the perfect rationalization for not accepting the responsibility for my behavior. This would be fine if it were not for the fact that I lose contact with myself when I suggest that I am not responsible for my actions. Besides losing self-consciousness, however, I am creating personal restrictions to my freedom.

Everyone is responsible for himself and his own increase, or lack of growth. As much as we would like to place the "blame" for lack of growth outside of ourselves, the truth remains with us — our own fear of responsibility and freedom restricts the growth process. We are not objects which can be manipulated; but rather free and responsible human beings in the process of becoming the kind of person we most want to be.

If a person is going to be genuine in his relationship with others, his actions must have a certain fundamental spontaneity about them. In order to reach an authenticity which is a result of a certain naturalness there must be little deliberation before acting. When we meet a person who enjoys this spontaneity which precedes so naturally from some individuals, we cannot but be impressed by the ease with which his words and actions so readily flow from the heart. It is as if each thought, idea, or action expressed was a result of the person's looking inside of himself and expressing what he finds there with a freedom that was not limited by the reactions of others.

Freedom of thought and movement is seriously desired by everyone, but the terrible sense of responsibility which would be a result of such spontaneity makes this freedom a goal only half sought in our daily activities. In order to justify our lack of honesty with ourselves and others, we must also suggest a series of rationalizations. To admit we fear the responsibility for our actions before others would be to admit a basic weakness of character. Therefore, persons normally look to their family or job responsibilities to supply necessary excuses for their lack of personal honesty. By adding to the personal structures most work presents by its very nature, it is easy to be swept up in a tide which will see the individual surrendering initiative in greater and greater degrees until they see themselves losing their identity in an attempt to attain a security and escape responsibility.

From a religious as well as a human point of view, the standpoint which may well give man the most significant insight into himself is that from which he is allowed to view himself in relation to his own freedom. There is no desire to make such freedom unlimited, but it appears that to the extent one understands the freedom intrinsic to man he understands man. To say the same thing under the light of personal subjectivity, man understands himself as a sequence of events freely chosen. When he reflects on these events even superficially, he discovers that there is no way to hold them together through logic or external norms. To explain their emergence at all, he must view them as a sequence of personal decisions growing out of his internal ability to choose when and how he will act.

If a man is willing to accept himself as a free agent, then he must realize the uniqueness of his experience. From the infinity of choices with which man is constantly confronted, he makes a path for himself which is fundamentally unique. Such a path has never before been traveled by any man nor will it be repeated in the course of human history.

In view of the unique choices which life offers to the free man, the weakness of allowing oneself to be determined by other factors is that much more significant. The man who chooses to deny the freedom which is fundamental to his experience is perverting his existence by looking outside himself for factors which will determine his existence and release him from the responsibilities of freedom. If freedom is as fundamental as human experience would lead us to believe, then the use of this freedom in order to escape responsibility is that much more perverse. The sad fact is, however, that man may just as easily renounce freedom as he may accept its challenge to move creatively along patterns which produce growth.

It is not surprising to discover men taking the line of least resistance when confronted with their own freedom. The ultimate decision to face one's own freedom is difficult enough without society's entering into the picture and making such decisions that much more difficult. Under the guise of "getting things done" and "getting them done efficiently," society moves in ways which force the individual to conform to the norms of the group for values which lie outside of the human value system. In order to increase the gross national product, for example, society will regulate the actions of the individual in his work. When the gross national product has become more important than the individuals attempting to increase it, however, the society has begun to make freedom inaccessible to the individual.

If we reflect on the example of the child's fear of being different from "all the other children," we see that our Western society tends to establish conformity as one of its values. When we see a child standing shamefaced before a group because of his fear of ridicule, we observe an atomistic unit which witnesses to our society's tendency to mold all into identical units in order to escape the "bother" of having to understand individual differences. As the military-industrial ideal grows and becomes more accepted by our society generally, we will gradually witness the death of the creative and imaginative. A society which moves to establish some kind of uniform behavior for all to follow generates more and more frustration for the person attempting to assert that freedom with which he was born and without which he will not be able to fulfill himself.

Though a significant amount of energy is expended in an effort to reveal to others an "ideal self" which we think will be acceptable to others, our true self is ultimately discerned by all and accepted or rejected on its own merits. Since so much of our time is spent in creating this "ideal self," little effort is spent in pursuits which naturally flow from the real person we are when we act spontaneously. We have all experienced the free flow of self-expression during our lives which makes it difficult to understand the reason for spending so much effort in protecting ourselves from honest expression.

The Church's laws inhibit freedom in those who will misinterpret them. The person who looks to negative laws in order to discover the positive fulfillment which is fundamental to Christianity is reducing any chance he might have of living the authentic and spontaneous life. Ironically, many are restricted by the laws of the Church in their attempt to discover the love Christ preached in the gospel.

It would certainly be a tragic thing to discover more freedom outside the Church than one could find in it. No matter how much one might want to hide from the fact, Christians are looking outside the Church to better understand the freedom which is consistently obvious. St. Paul spoke eloquently of freedom within the Church, but the finest interpretations of this freedom have not traditionally come from the men who live within the walls of the Church Paul risked his life to defend. Despite the manifest freedom of Christ and the message he preached to the world, the Church has become all too active in identifying men with an identity which minimizes individual differences.

If we are ever going to identify the Church with the freedom which was Christ's basic message to mankind, it is important to rid ourselves of a static concept of man. When man knows that within the Church "responding to the Christian message" means living according to a predetermined mode of behavior, he cannot be expected to hold much esteem for the Church or its values. It is strange to note that the Church which is identified with the doctrine of free will also preaches that a common natural law restricts the actions of all men.

In order to place man in the atmosphere which is conducive to growth, we must drop all notions which suggest that he is stripped of individuality. The Church tends to project, by contrast, the image of man so limited in means to attain individuality that few can identify with it. If our common experience means anything, it is that we do not identify with an image of ourselves reduced to an essential nature attempting to regulate life according to fixed norms.

Far more than adding the accidental to our nature, however, we must express our communion with others in order to express adequately our own self-concept. Any honest attempt to discover ourselves in this manner will express our communion with others as a significant part of ourselves. If we were to remove others from our world, we would necessarily lose our chances for self-expression.

Each person makes constant contact with others. In making such contact, all are able to personally grow and allow others to grow depending on the quality of the relationship. When the contact with a free man generates a level of communication which truly expresses the depths of that man, we can be sure that there is a communal growth toward which all men aspire. To neglect the range of experience which becomes a part of us as the result of contacting other free men is to neglect a genuine part of man in his attempt to understand himself.

To those who lack the experience of making contact with men who may be best described as centers of freedom, the need for such contact may seem to be superficial. In the eyes of such men, contact with others usually means nothing more than familiarity. If one has met an individual at a cocktail party, had dinner and shared a few experiences with him, he feels he knows that man as deeply as he cares to. One who does not descend beneath this level of familiarity either because he does not care to or because he fears the consequences will not reach the level of intimacy which makes relationships between persons genuinely meaningful.

The kind of person who prides himself on the number of friends he can claim without any apparent regard for the quality of the friendship, normally places a great deal of importance on his ability to adjust to any group. Whether or not such a person would admit it, the ability to adjust to the group gradually becomes the outstanding personal accomplishment in his life. If such a person could only become conscious of the manner in which such attempts at "adjustment" begin to erode the boundaries of freedom, he would never claim it as an accomplishment. With the group norms the primary goal of an individual, it is not difficult to see how freedom becomes an empty and sterile form of existence.

In his attempt to sense and adjust to the norms of the majority surrounding him at any given time, a person can become a slave in his desire for conformity. From a desire to seek an apparent good, the person gradually destroys his own uniqueness. If we see nothing beyond the norms of the group as meaningful for ourselves, then it is possible that we have allowed the group to substitute for some of our vital freedom.

It certainly takes no profound insight to be able to articulate the negative aspects that groups tend to adopt when they are only superficially aware of themselves, but it is important to recall from time to time the real situation. Groups naturally tend to want to "get things done" and will throw themselves into what they believe is their primary purpose without even momentary reflection upon whether or not the goals suggested have any meaning for them as individuals. Only after much work in attempting to achieve certain goals will the persons who make up a group begin to question where they are going and why they have chosen particular means to arrive there. When allowed to reflect momentarily in the very beginning, groups will, however, realize that most attempts to "get things done" are another attempt to hide from consciousness the real goals that each individual has for himself and the group.

A final example of negative goals groups generally tend toward in their attempt to hide from themselves is the tendency toward togetherness. By being together, many will fool themselves into thinking they are achieving fellowship. In most instances of togetherness, however, one discovers within its framework another avenue of escape from the quality of sharing each fundamentally desires within his own life. Rather than admit the desire to fill a gap created by loneliness, people will deceive themselves into thinking they are not alone when surrounded by others.

*   *   *

The rationale for introducing group dynamics into retreats originated from this total philosophy of man. If one were to ignore the subject for reasons which did not spring from the same level of meaning, he would be extremely superficial in his approach. While there would be no attempt to hide the fact that many would hope to pass over the subject without reflecting to the depths of such a discussion, there is no escape from the fact that, far more than just introducing another exercise into the retreat, those who advocate group dynamics are attempting to change the entire atmosphere of the retreat itself.

If one is in sympathy with the description of man which has been presented, he simply cannot fail to see the frustration which present retreat formats cause the individual searching for growth in the Christian life. One would be hiding from reality to ignore the fact that traditional retreat formats effectively block attempts to personally confront Christ. If man is anything like the description presented earlier, then it would appear the retreat does little more than inhibit growth.

In the dimension of spiritual growth, the classical retreat format might very well be considered a well-meaning concentration camp. If one were to compare the concentration camp with the retreat by analogy, it would reveal some striking parallels on the psychological level. The insistence on absolute silence during the entire period of retreat, for example, closely simulates the solitary confinement of the prison. While the reasons for such silence are obviously more exalted in the retreat, the fact remains that by choosing to end communication between persons for a prolonged period of time, many of the same effects of confinement will be stimulated. There is no doubt that individuals desperately need the solitude which retreat may offer, but it appears to be an extreme to suggest that if a little silence is good, total silence must be better. Man normally works out his salvation in and through others. It would appear obvious that the inspirations gathered during solitude could be best integrated with others who are in the same process of self-examination. If we were to attempt to discover a means to discourage the possible effect of an inspiration gathered, none might be suggested which would better accomplish the task than to refuse the one inspired the opportunity to share it with another.

Another example of good prison tactics which finds an obvious application within the retreat format is the passivity of the role of listener. One would have to be clever indeed to devise a method of better insulating someone from himself. To be out of communication with others in one's surroundings and be constantly in the role of listener creates an atmosphere of frustration for the normal individual who wants to articulate ideas with others in order to assimilate them in the context of reality. The individual is forced in the atmosphere of silence to accept ideas without ultimately testing them in the light of reality which sharing implies.

The overall effect of a large number of retreatants sitting through the same talks combined with a background of silence and identical religious exercises appears to be similar to the mass production of food and goods which has become such an intimate part of the American scene. The retreat master may give the same talks to thousands of retreatants without altering anything in his production. Without regard for the differences between this group of retreatants and the last, retreat after retreat may be produced in much the same manner that the assembly line produces similar products by the thousands. The retreat master must constantly strive to gain insight into this particular group for whom he is giving this particular retreat. Otherwise, he may easily lapse into a feeling of security by the easy manner in which all groups may appear to be similarly inspired by the same group of talks. Insulated from one another and thus unconscious of any common reaction to what is being said or done, the retreatant has no genuine way of offering effective response to the retreat master in order to make the experience one which would produce maximum growth. Under such environmental conditions, changes in the format or concept of retreats will have to be slow in developing. The day has finally come, however, when those subjected to the old retreat format have found their voice and the courage to plead for a retreat atmosphere which has more growth potential than that previously experienced.

If the retreat itself is to be something worth experiencing, it must demonstrate that love exists between persons because it is on the love experience that the entire Christian life is based. Christ expressed in his words and actions the theme of love as the center of life. From this central love expression of the

Christian message, all other themes of Christianity emerge. Without coming from this center of charity, our Christian activity cannot help but be ultimately frustrating.

If we apply this to retreats, it can be seen that the more the atmosphere is conducive to expressed love the more productive the retreat will ultimately become. In an atmosphere of imposed silence protracted over a period of days, there is obviously a limited opportunity to get to know persons in the retreat better, let alone beginning the hard work of understanding them and sharing a common bond of friendship and love. When at least part of the retreat time is given over to sharing with one another the frustrations, joys, sorrows and excitement which are individually unique in the life of each person attempting to follow the Christian life, there is more opportunity to draw close to one another and know something of the sense of Christian community experienced in apostolic times.

While there is no certainty that verbal communication will draw people closer during the time of retreat, it certainly follows that persons have less opportunity for sharing when isolated from one another by total silence. If we firmly believe special graces flow during the time of retreat, we should take special pains to make sure that there is opportunity to exercise these and not let the delicate movement be stifled by insulation. It would seem that only those who are satisfied with the filling station model of grace could accept the absolute silence during retreat. If the time of retreat is the stop at the filling station which enables one to run the rest of the year on the fuel stored at that time, it is then reasonable to accept a retreat silence in order to make sure one had filled the tank with as much fuel as possible. If grace is better understood by comparing it to a fleeting inspiration or subtle insight, however, it will be best nurtured with the help of others. By insights gained through similar inspiration, others will take the time and trouble to help clarify the subtleties implicit in this delicate kind of insight. Such sharing will help make the inspiration a real part of the person before it slips away like a dream which is not immediately reflected upon after waking.

When we consider the fact that each person on retreat has a lifetime of experience to share, the crime of frustrating attempts to share this potential is all the more unrealistic. Not only is a life of experience available, but a life of attempts to integrate the secular and Christian. If we are truly living according to the norms established by Christ, we are constantly experiencing a tension between our selfish and unselfish attempts to discover ultimate meaning in our path through life. Those who have taken the effort to make retreat a part of this life are obviously making serious attempts to integrate the Christian message into all aspects of their lives. If we do not make available the experiences of others which have been fulfilling as well as those which have been frustrating, our lack of sharing will make the retreat period that much less a source of knowledge and grace.

It is perfectly obvious that each person's experience is different from that of every other person. This is particularly true in the case of individuals attempting to make the Christian message meaningful in their day-to-day life. If we were to take any gospel passage, for example, and ask individuals what this passage meant in terms of their daily lives, the difference in the interpretations would be startling. This merely attests to the fact that scripture penetrates much beneath doctrine to the real core of life in the person who will reflectively consider its contents.

If we were to attempt to point to one of the most significant goals expected from introducing group discussion into the retreat format, it would be to blend the many experiential differences into a unified theme which would allow us to more completely integrate Christ's teaching into our own life. Any group of persons will begin from divergent points of view in relation to the meaning of religion in their lives, but a free atmosphere of discussion will allow them to integrate their apparent differences into a single vision. If we truly believe that Christ came to preach the word of salvation to all men, we would readily accept the fact that there would be as many outlooks on the message as there are unique human beings receiving that same message. However, we also have to admit an apparent paradox — that the message besides speaking to each man individually is unified in its basic theme. To move toward finding and revealing the unifying theme should be the aim of an inspired retreat experience.

By sharing personal experiences and working together with others to unify their ideas, those involved in a retreat find it has a personal significance rather than being a collection of statements which are meaningful to some and irrelevant to others. By sharing with others in an attempt to find meaning from apparently unconnected experience, each draws closer to an acceptance of the end result by the very fact that he played some integral role in the action of the group. Rather than listening to one person's interpretation of Christ's message to man in a completely passive manner, the retreatant becomes actively engaged in sharing with others and attempting to integrate his thoughts into his own attempt to understand the Word revealed to men.

In this active manner, the mystery is returned to the search for religious meaning in life. If there was anything implicit in Christ's words and actions, it was the mystery in religion. His words constantly lend themselves to new insights which develop within the minds of the reflective. As time goes by and we gain new knowledge in other fields, our understanding of Christ's words increases and the gospel becomes more profound in its implications. When we are able to more actively involve men in the quest for the truth in the gospel message, it seems we should be anxious to move toward such involvement rather than shrink from it.

If we really believe in man's basic freedom and that we commit men more deeply to truth by incorporating this freedom into the search, then we must accept the fact that this questioning spirit prompts him to probe the mystery of faith. Only a belief that our faith contains no mystery and is rather presented to us in neat packets of knowledge would stifle the attempt to explore. If Christ's intention was to end the search, he could certainly have chosen much different terms in which to convey his message. His phrases rather prompt exploration by their very ambiguity. After reading a particular scriptural passage, one is struck by the fact that Christ is so clearly able to answer profound questions with such clarity. Reflecting more deeply on the responses, however, creates a sense of wonder. While it is not the negative kind of doubt which implies that the answer may not be correct, it is a doubt which invites more exploration. In order to probe the depths of the Christian message in this sense, the introduction of exchange in the retreat format is suggested. If we believe that the gospel has a depth which can never be completely known by man and that free man exploring ever deeper into the meaning contained therein will ultimately become more committed to Christ's teaching, nothing would fulfill the goals of Christianity better than to teach, wherever and whenever possible, the best manner of exploring the message.

3.   group dynamics

When one uses the term "leader" in our society today, the concepts of responsibility and authority immediately spring to the minds of most people.[1] From the common experience of seeing leaders chosen in the fields of business, education, industry, and the military, we have come to think of choosing leaders by discovering persons who are able to "take charge" of situations or "handle" people in difficult situations. One might say that we look for leaders who will be able to persuade persons to think along the same lines as the leader.[2] For a society to function smoothly, it is important for us to have businessmen who will be able to instill the goals of the corporation into the value system of those working for them; to have teachers who will be able to train students to accept the thoughts and ideas of the great minds who have been accepted by society, or to have military officers who will be able to command the respect of his men in order that they will be able to efficiently and effectively accept the orders passed on.

If we turn the same concept around, we find that those looking to leaders for direction expect to become dependent on the wisdom, courage, intelligence, and self-sufficiency of the man chosen to lead. It is not for the soldier to question the orders given to him, the factory worker to question the goals of the corporation, or the student to wonder about the material taught to him. If the leader is to operate effectively within this framework, it is important for him to be able to create an image such that those in his charge will draw their strength, direction, goals, and even their value system from him. If the persons under a leader begin to look to their own inner resources, they

43

may find themselves in conflict with those of the leader and create discord in attempts to realize the goals determined for the group.

Modern psychology has recently questioned our rather stable concept of leadership. By evaluating the goals of groups as well as the reflections of those participating in groups as non-leaders, there seems to be sufficient evidence to suggest that our present concept of leadership is not as effective as it appears on the surface.

If one were to attempt to sum up the direction of the findings presented thus far by investigators, it would have to be a statement which suggested that group leadership might be better carried out by the entire group rather than any individual in the group.[3] Such a statement can be confusing and apparently contradictory to the uninitiated. If one can imagine leadership as a set of many functions rather than a singular function, the stage would be set for understanding the manner in which such leadership might exist. If we can destroy the concept of leader as a role to be played by an individual and begin to conceptualize leadership in an abstract manner which would define it as a set of functions to be performed within a group, we would be well on our way to discovering the modern use of the term leader.

If such leadership is going to exist within a given group, it is important that each individual fulfill a unique function to see to it that the group as a whole is able to define its role, clarify its questions, or solve its problems.[4] If the members of the group sense that they themselves are responsible for the success or failure of the group goals, then they will begin to assume the individual function necessary to assure the movement and direction of the group. When this kind of responsibility is not reflected in each individual, such a need to participate actively will not develop.

In the sense that he tends to accept personally the responsibility for the results of group action, the traditional leader does not allow the ultimate potential of each individual to be released in its most complete form. The leader who either implicitly or explicitly removes the responsibility for the results from the group actually impedes the dynamic qualities which surround the most successful groups. Since our concepts of leadership have been a part of our lives for so long, it is difficult for us to realize that by "taking charge" of the group a leader may actually impede progress.

If the leader's function is not to take responsibility for the group by suggesting the goals for the group, the most effective means to attain those goals, the best-prepared persons to perform the many actions which must be executed, and other roles normally afforded to the leader, one might readily question just what the leader's function can and should be. The group which is functioning most effectively and efficiently according to modern psychologists is primarily doing everything that will effect the diffusion of leadership throughout the group. While it is understandable that each leader may use different "techniques" for accomplishing the goal of diffuse leadership, it is important that the leader do everything within his capacity to accomplish this goal.

Another way of saying the same thing is to suggest that the effective leader creates the conditions in which his image of leadership will be lost as rapidly as possible.[5] Many educators at least pay lip service to the same kind of movement. Significant persons in the field of education have stated that the effective teacher is the one who allows his students to grow to the point that they no longer need the support of an instructor and are prepared to strike out on their own.

In trying to move toward a group-centered leadership, many leaders make completely unrealistic attempts which are doomed to failure from the beginning. A leader who *tells* a group that they are now responsible for the action of the group and by his actions points to the fact that such a concept is not understood or accepted by him, would have been more effective if he had not suggested the idea in the first place. Persons are so accustomed to having someone else make the decisions and assume the responsibility that it is not surprising when they are not ready to assume immediate leadership and must be, in fact, brought to this concept very gradually. To think that such a subtle concept of leadership will be accomplished by *fiat* is to sadly miss the point of the entire discussion.

If our group-centered leader will begin the first discussion with the attitude that he is to be no more than a participant observer, he will have made the first great step toward assuming his correct stance in relation to the other members in the group. He should use all of his personal talents to assure the members of the group that he really intends his function to be that of a group member. If it seems that the leader's duty to assume the role of participant is difficult, it will be that much more difficult to suggest that role to the participant. Persons are so accustomed to rejecting any responsibility for the actions of a group that the concrete implications of such responsibility are not only difficult to assume but even to conceptualize.

In allowing the members of the group the freedom to assume their leadership in this manner, the group-centered leader can genuinely assume responsibility. The leader must "teach" the members to assume the leadership functions proper to the group. As will be seen in the development of the topic, the teaching role will not be traditional. More by his trust, confidence, and attitudes generally than by any specific word content, he will be able to "teach" the kind of leadership which will allow the group to attain its maximum potential.

Such a concept of leadership is so foreign to our thinking that it is natural to question the exact manner in which the leader can ever hope to accomplish the goals suggested. In a real sense, it is difficult to attempt to conceptualize the manner in which this will be accomplished. This is particularly true since, as was suggested, the role can only be assumed through correct use of attitudes and emotions. While such attitudes may be described in detail, many are not able to assume such attitudes toward a group of persons and will not be successful in their attempts to create diffusion of the leader's roles.

If there is a foundation upon which a group will build its own self-awareness, it is the confidence of the leader in the basic capacities of the group. To the extent that the leader believes the group is better able to solve their own problems than the leader himself, there will be genuine movement toward unleashing the dynamic upon which successful groups are established. The leader who does not believe in the work he is attempting to accomplish will necessarily be unsuccessful. Since such a concept of leadership relies heavily on the emotional awareness of the members' own abilities, any hidden reservations on part of the leader will be sensed by group. Any ambivalence of the leader between what he is saying and what he is thinking will be discovered by the group sufficiently to make the entire attempt a failure.

Another attitude which is very much like the trust in the ability of the group is the complete willingness of the leader to respect all opinions which are expressed. Since the leader is to be a genuine participant within the group setting, it is unrealistic for him not to have his own unique feelings about the particular matter being discussed. Any members of the group who feel that their opinions are being distorted by the leader in order to "direct" the group to the leader's solution to the problem, however, will undoubtedly be handicapped in attempting to release their basic potential. It would be far better for the leader to openly declare that his solution was the one the group must accept than to attempt subtle manipulation of the members toward his own unique solution. By consistent and unwavering respect for each person's opinions the leader will be able to move others toward respect for one another's opinions which is one of the most significant goals than can be achieved by any group.

There is a very subtle difference between this respect for the opinions of others and the personal freedom to express my own opinions which may run contrary to those of the group. In an attempt to respect the opinions of all, the leader might fall into the fundamental error of losing his own identity. There is quite a difference between fear that my own opinions might be rejected and manipulation of others' opinions to satisfy my own desire to "lead" them to my "superior" manner of thinking.

Between those two diametrically opposed attitudes, however, lies the attitude which will free the group for the most significant and creative thinking they can provide.

Though this attitude can be genuinely conceived as narrow, it might also be discovered to be broad in that any emotion which transfers a sense of trust to the group will be growth facilitating. The reason that the image of narrowness immediately occurs is that seldom does a leader genuinely display trust in those to whom he relates. In many subtle ways, a leader is constantly attempting to manipulate others so that they will "realize" the wisdom of his opinions. Unfortunately, the human person is constructed in such a way that he is extremely sensitive to such manipulation and interprets it personally to the extent that he loses much personal confidence in the manipulating. In the process, leaders may be able to regulate behavior, but not basic attitudes. When this occurs, our group member is engaged in an activity which is not a part of himself and necessarily lacks much in its execution.

If one claims that such trust and respect for the opinions of others comes very naturally to him, it is because he has blocked himself from an awareness of the genuine tension which develops as the result of conflict between the action which I "know" a group "must" take and those actions which they will tend to examine when unchallenged by controls from others. While such personal conflict may develop from an unnecessary sense of responsibility for the direction a group may choose, this does not eliminate the conflict which results as a necessary conclusion to such responsibility, whether real or imaginary. In the coping which allows the leader to live with such conflict, he is taking the greatest single step toward moving the group in a positive direction. It would not be an overstatement to suggest that the leader will be successful to the extent that he can control his personal sense of fear and responsibility which naturally evolves as a result of his role in allowing group members their freedom of expression.

*   *   *

In order to emphasize the same points from another perspective it might prove valuable to examine the group from the vantage point of the participating members.[6] The primary freedom which should be sensed by the members on the deepest level is the freedom to participate or not participate as they are inclined. One who is aware of the inhibitions within the average person which prevent his honesty with others will begin to appreciate the reason he must be so sensitive to all factors which might increase any person's uneasiness. If the leader transfers to a group member a lack of trust, there is no doubt that the individual member will also lack a freedom in expression which will result in an incomplete experience for everyone.

Persons generally lack respect for themselves. And it is not surprising that any lack of respect shown by the leader will be magnified by the individual member to the extent that he basically doubts his own value. Because the individual is normally inhibited in self-expression due to his doubt about the value of what he might say, any reinforcement by the leader will compound the inhibitions to the spontaneity necessary if the group is to realize its potential.

While experience alone will fundamentally assure any leader of the reality, it will be stated that fear of members usurping power from the leader in a nonthreatening atmosphere is basically unfounded. Though many have expressed the same kind of doubts, persons in a position of leadership who have been able to transmit a genuine sense of trust and respect for each person and his opinion do not find group members anxious or even willing to take over the leadership and reduce the leader to a noneffective position. Quite to the contrary, members who have been assured that they will be respected as individuals will most likely turn with greater willingness to the opinion and judgment of the leader in his honest attempt to maximize the experience for all concerned.

One thing which prevents groups from communicating effectively with one another is their unresolved interpersonal conflicts which subtly nullify any honest attempts to come to grips with the apparent problem before the group.[7] If one member dislikes another for any reason, it would be next to impossible for him to agree on a given point, no matter how logical, for fear that such agreement might be interpreted as defeat on the interpersonal level. Until the more fundamental level of conflict comes honestly to the fore, discussion of ideas will be seriously impeded possibly to the point of a stalemate. Such lack of effective solutions to group problems may be very subtle since open expression of discontent could also be a personal revelation which the individual might find threatening. If, for example, a member of a given group makes me angry for a logical or emotional reason, and I do not express that resentment, it will grow until the expression of my anger may seriously injure another person. On the other hand, if I can honestly express my anger when I first begin to feel it I have a much better chance of growing positively and in harmony with each person toward the goals chosen by the group.

Such a calm expression of feeling before it grows out of proportion will be the greatest step toward clarifying misunderstandings and eliminating personal conflict which could hamper the more important work toward which the group is attempting to orient itself. One who argues that there is no necessity for eliminating purely personal conflict in order to build an effective group relation might well construct a perfectly consistent argument. If faced with answering such a possible objection, the response would have to attack the premise upon which it is based.

The final statement which should be made from the authoritative standpoint is, therefore, that those recognized for their sensitivity to the inner workings of groups have felt that groups will most efficiently and effectively be creative in an atmosphere which allows them to eliminate their interpersonal conflicts before attempting to take on the more apparent goals of the group.

If one were to attempt a description of the atmosphere which must surround persons who are attempting to be free in their relations with others, he would describe it as nonthreatening.[8] A climate in which he discovers at least one person who unconditionally accepts him as a person will give the individual group member something of the personal security necessary to risk himself and his identity in order to express himself at an emotional level. When one or more members of the group do not evoke judgment of him as an individual implicitly by their comments, a freedom will grow within the group which could not be otherwise present. When members of the group begin to make honest attempts to understand the basic meaning of things expressed rather than looking for logical flaws in such expressions, a climate is created which will allow each member to probe into the area of conflict for him rather than superficially commenting on such conflict which more often than not causes unnecessary blocks to genuine understanding. All of this is another way of saying that when the climate is nonthreatening, the chance of genuine growth for the members is increased far beyond any normal expectations.

*   *   *

While the descriptive attempts thus far may be helpful for one who genuinely desires to create such a climate in his work with groups, it does not really give him guidelines for such work. One may understand well the need to be accepting, non-judgmental, and understanding in his relationship with persons in order to create conditions favorable to their growth and still be at a loss to know the manner in which he might display such attitudes. Though attempts at description again fall short because of the emotional content which is implicit in such attitudes, a more specific attempt will be directed at relating the functions a group-centered leader must perform in order to create the climate desired.

All work done in the field of group dynamics emphasizes the necessity of warmth and empathy. The leader who cannot convey empathy to the group might as well not begin any attempts to unleash the dynamic which is implicit when a group gathers. Unfortunately for the writer, it is far easier to sense a warm person than to describe one. From common experience, we know that some persons are described as warm and others are not. If we were to ask anyone why they describe another as warm, they are more often than not at a loss for adequate words. This does not, however, hinder them from being confident of their description.

In order to begin to describe a warm and empathetic person, we might choose to focus on the person who lacks these qualities. In relating to one who is cold toward us, we see certain qualities which are most easily described. If a personal conflict exists in us we sense a certain stiffness in his manner when in his presence. To further identify this feeling we also sense ourselves becoming stiff in our manner, gesture, and expression in his presence. Remarks are, more often than not, superficial in their content and in their vague implications. As in the case of describing a personality which emanates warmth, the person who is unfriendly may be easily sensed although not so readily described.

To move to those personality characteristics which are normally part of a person who is described as warm one might point to his spontaneity. This person does not have a great number of façades and defenses which block his personality from emerging. For a leader to be free to expose himself with such spontaneity is to attract others in the same direction. By joining this quality with a natural tendency to empathize with others, the members of any given group will begin to feel comfortable in the presence of such a leader. It is impossible at this time to attempt a judgment concerning the real effect of such a leader on the members of a group, but it does appear that such tendencies toward spontaneity and empathy create a nonthreatening environment which allows more freedom of expression than was previously possible.

Without anything like a complete understanding of the dynamics involved in the process, there is evidence to suggest that group members begin to behave toward one another as the leader behaves toward them. If the leader is warm and friendly in his relations toward members of the group, the members of the group begin to relate to one another in the same manner.

A group may begin with no one but the leader offering warmth and understanding to the members of the group, but his consistency in this attitude will gradually influence the members toward similar behavior. When such an attitude becomes prevalent in the group, an atmosphere is created which facilitates communication and understanding which are the foundations upon which group goals are most easily attained.[9]

If we were to examine the average group at the beginning of any given experience, we would note the inability to listen to one another. We would note persons responding to one another before they had understood the import of the question or statement just related. If one were to attempt a dynamic description of such responses, he would probably suggest that the individual who was supposed to be listening was not so much listening to what was being asked as formulating a reply to the question he thought was going to be asked. Two persons apparently communicating with one another are often carrying on two conversations without being aware for some time that they are not really "tuned in" to one another.

This entire syndrome becomes more obvious to the individual when he recalls personal experiences in this area. On many occasions during the average lifetime, one finds himself a spectator during an argument between two other persons. For one reason or another, the argument generates no particular emotional content at the time. He is really able to listen in a detached manner to both sides of the argument and after some short period of time he becomes aware that the two individuals arguing are really not disagreeing at all. In many such cases there is not only a lack of disagreement, but those arguing are really talking about two entirely different things.

In much the same way our detached observer is in a position to give those arguing an objective vantage point which will eliminate conflict, the leader should at all times be in a position to describe to the members of the group the fundamental dynamics involved in any discussion.[10] The leader cannot afford to remain aloof from the members of the group, but he can strive to keep himself from being emotionally involved in the discussion to the point of losing perspective of the total interaction of the group. By really listening sensitively to each person and showing ultimate respect for the opinions expressed, the leader not only gains personal perspective but also serves as an example to others in their attempts to understand themselves and their relations to others.

If a leader is to be really effective in this area, he must be constantly aware of more than just the verbal content of any given statement. We often find, for example, persons relating what would appear to be a rather neutral event and becoming emotionally choked in the process. To respond to the content and not the emotion would be to miss the dynamic present at that time. The leader who is to be successful at all in his attempts to release people from their fears and façades which block communication must be extremely sensitive to the basic ambiguity between what people say and what they mean. To a greater or lesser degree this ambiguity prevails in all persons. In order to release the dynamic, one must be aware and able to articulate such awareness to others.

One thing which will reduce a leader's effectiveness is a fear of allowing the group to proceed at its own pace in its own direction. The leader who has predetermined ideas as to the direction the group must move and an impatience to move in that direction cannot help but transfer this feeling to others. If there is "not enough time" to discover the emotional obstacles preventing free movement, surely no one will begin the difficult task of revealing himself in order to acquire such freedom. When the leader has a basic impatience with the movement of the group, he simply cannot be warm and accepting toward those who are blocked from such movement temporarily. The most important thing for the effective leader is the acceptance of the group members not only as persons but also as persons in their present movement or lack of movement.

There is no doubt that impatience with the group will inhibit the more important emotions the leader should display toward group members, but it also follows that under such conditions the leader cannot be really sensitive to the difference between the meaning and intent behind statements made. Any given statement may be a veiled attempt to say something quite different from the verbal content it projects. In order to discover the difference between the meaning and intent in such statements, a leader must be acutely aware of the difference between the expression used by the speaker and the overall impression he is conveying. As a leader becomes more aware of the group in process, the more he will be able to sense fear, anger, sorrow, and other emotions which lie at the base of apparently unemotional statements made throughout a discussion. To the extent that he is able to articulate this awareness to the group, he will be successful in creating an atmosphere of growth conducive to the goal for which a group is striving.

If one were to attempt to sum up the goal of the leader in a concise phrase, it would be the ability to adopt the internal frame of reference from which the speaker is operating. The leader must not only be acutely aware of what words are being used but actually attempt to internalize the emotions of the speaker which prompt such statements. The leader must actually attempt to "get inside the skin" of another human being. Though any attempt to become so aware of the internal feelings of another human being is impossible, real progress along this line can be made by anyone willing to make sincere efforts. From honest attempts to "become another person," one can actually sense, at some depth, the feelings, emotions, and intellectual vantage point from which another is operating at any given time.

The leader who is successful in his attempts to articulate the impression made by a speaker as well as to understand his expression will also make others more sensitive to such a distinction. As such an awareness grows, so will the honesty of the group members toward one another. If the group members become aware of the fact that they are speaking to persons who are able to sense ambiguities in expression, they soon realize they must speak honestly or not speak at all. If a feeling of warmth and acceptance grows along with the sensitive awareness, individuals will become more and more secure in expressing their honest feelings and probing the depths of these feelings openly with progressively less fear and more freedom.

In order for any group to honestly begin to reach its goals there must be an ability on the part of the leader to convey acceptance. Without the feeling of acceptance being generated by at least one person in the group, there is little hope that the group members will be able to work effectively toward their goals in a free atmosphere most conducive to creative progress. In order to accomplish this it is necessary for the leader to remain constantly aware of the group's position at all times. If the group is bewildered, confused, and at an apparent standstill, it is important for the leader to remain with them in this confusion until they are able to naturally overcome the obstacles to communication. To press the group beyond their confusion toward the goals with which the leader is preoccupied would be to leave an unresolved doubt which can be a permanent block to generating a solution which would adequately reflect the personal involvement of all.

If we are to adequately reflect reality within the context of this discussion, we must be aware of the "limits" our acceptance can take. A leader is often limited by boundaries set by those outside of the discussion — principals, superiors, etc. There are those limits beyond which the leader cannot allow the group to stray and still remain genuinely accepting toward the group. In order to maximize his acceptance of the group, each leader must strive to become clear about the limits set by himself and others. A leader who suggests that a given limit to any discussion is generated from outside but the members of the group sense that this is rather a personal limitation imposed by the lack of freedom in the leader will appear dishonest in his relationship to the group and not worthy of their trust. When the leader takes an entirely different tack, however, and points to the limitation as something he cannot allow for a given reason, the members will be better able to accept this and consequently feel closer to the leader because of his honesty, though they might personally feel unnecessarily restricted by such a limitation.

The last of the important functions which the leader must

perform in order to make a group conscious of the direction in which they are tending in a discussion is often referred to as a "linking" function. By the "linking" function, we are referring to the ability of the group leader to tie together statements made by the group so that the members begin to become conscious of the overall direction the discussion is taking. Without someone to adopt a vantage point above the discussion, the individual statements may apparently be random comments which do not pertain to one another. "Linking" the statements together in some meaningful way which makes others conscious of their flow puts the individual members in a much better position to add significantly to or counter the collective thought of the group.

If one were to attempt to tie this concept of "linking" to previously comments, it would be most closely aligned with the goal of discovering meaning and intent in a given statement. Opposed to discovering the genuine meaning behind the individual statement, however, this function is an attempt to discover the meaning the group is attempting to suggest collectively. Some may react skeptically to the possibility of a group expression, but experience would indicate that groups act like individuals in many ways and can easily express themselves in much the same manner as individuals. With someone conscious of the subtleties involved in the process, they are able to communicate a clear and precise statement of their collective thinking on any given topic.

If we were to attempt to point to the one significant characteristic of group dynamics it would appear it is the fact that the members of the group grow more and more like the leader in their attitudes, actions, and values. If the leader is conscious of this, his responsibility becomes great. He must be sure he relates to the group members as he expects them to relate to him and to one another. It is incumbent upon the leader to evaluate his fundamental goals for the group and make himself consciously aware of his own ability to achieve these goals before hoping to aid others in such growth.

* * *

In order to round out this chapter on the group process, it is necessary to summarize the outcomes which one can reasonably expect from a group which has had sensitive and meaningful leadership. The leader who has been effective in creating an atmosphere which is basically nonthreatening can rest assured that the members of the group will feel they are accepted. By projecting an attitude toward the members which is warm, nonjudgmental, and emphatic, the leader can attract to himself persons who would ordinarily resist due to a fear of rejection. Under the proper conditions, members feel that people are attentive to them and are making every sincere effort to understand them.

Closely aligned to the feeling of being understood which members sense in a group where the basic dynamic has been released is the feeling of acceptance which is generated.[11] Contrary to the feeling of rejection most people fear if they speak honestly about any subject is the acceptance which they experience in an atmosphere which allows such honesty. One who broadens his perspective would realize that the feeling of acceptance also includes the feeling of security, spontaneity, and confidence which is either implicitly or explicitly expressed by those who sense acceptance by an individual or a group. From a negative point of view, the same people describe themselves as less defensive, less withdrawn, and less closed to experience than they have been at any other point in their lives.

The many expressions of acceptance which are a part of those who have had a meaningful group experience are expressions which would attest to the basic value of the group experience.

In order for a leader to measure the degree of acceptance which is part of a positive group experience, he need only measure the freedom to participate and communicate freely expressed by the members. The freedom to communicate is the necessary effect of the feeling of acceptance. When one feels free to communicate, he also feels accepted in the group which will accept his communication and vice versa. There is no such thing as having one without the other.

A common phenomenon observed among many persons is

their tendency to place the locus of self-evaluation outside of themselves.[12] In order to escape the responsibility for their actions, these people seek advice from others in order to shift the blame for anything which might go wrong in an attempt to escape guilt feelings. As a result of healthy group interaction, it has been noted that persons exhibit less and less of this behavior and begin to understand that no one else can accept the responsibility for their personal decision but themselves. Once they have come to make decisions as a result of personal reflection, they discover there is less guilt resulting from such decisions.

In order for members with an outside locus of evaluation to function, they must make some approximation as to the behavior necessary to please others. There is never any accurate way to predict those actions which will please another human being and the efforts to please others create a fear within the individual that his attempts are falling short of their mark. This can readily lead to a hostility toward others and ultimately force the person to lose contact with himself. In the proper setting, however, group members are seen to grow beyond this immature behavior and begin to realize that the only behavior which can ultimately be pleasing to others is that behavior which is genuinely a reflection of their own personality. Only when expressing this true personality to others can a person respond genuinely to others because his reactions of love, fear, joy, and sadness are the only human reactions he possesses.

Another result of expressing his own genuine reactions rather than a facade which is calculated to "manipulate" people into liking him is a growth of personal knowledge. By hiding from genuine reactions for so many years, persons lose sight of their unique individuality. After meaningful group relationships, members tend to understand themselves better and realize the intensity of their personal feelings. While they feared this honesty before, they now understand and appreciate how meaningful relationships can be when engaged in at this level.

As a result of coming into contact with themselves, persons become more conscious of the flow of life. By placing themselves in this flow, they become more conscious of the beauty around them. They become more aware of the sounds, color, and forms that surround them at any given time. They begin to "grow with the trees" in an indescribable manner, but with a consciousness of the grandeur which will be ultimately theirs. In its very best form, the group experience may only give one an insight into the process. The process is the full life in its most profound expression.

REFERENCES

1. Appreciation expressed for the basic outline of this chapter to: Gordon, Thomas. Group-centered leadership and administration. In Carl Rogers, *Client-Centered Therapy*. Boston: Houghton Mifflin, 1951.

2. Gibb, C. A. The research background of an interactional theory of leadership. *Australian Journal of Psychology*, 1950, 28, 19-42.

3. Preston, M. G. and Heintz, R. K. Effects of participatory vs. supervisory leadership on group judgment. *Journal of Abnormal and Social Psychology*, 1949, 44, 345-345.

4. Stogdill, R. M. Leadership, membership and organization. *Psychological Bulletin*, 1950, 47, 1-14.

5. Gordon, Thomas. Group-centered leadership and administration. In Carl R. Rogers, *Client-Centered Therapy*. Boston: Houghton Mifflin, 1951, 323-329.

6. Golden, C. S. and Ruttenberg, H. J. *The Dynamics of Industrial Democracy*. New York: Harper and Bros., 1942.

7. Gerard, H. B. The anchorage of opinions in face-to-face groups. *Human Relations*.

8. Bales, R. F. A theoretical framework for interaction process. In Robert Bales, *Interaction Process Analysis*. Cambridge: Addison-Wesley Press, 1950.

9. Homans, G. C. *The Human Group*. New York: Harcourt, Brace, 1950.

10. Reik, Theodor. *Listening with the Third Ear*. New York: Farrar, Straus, 1948.

11. Gordon, Thomas. What is gained by group participation. *Educational Leadership*, 1950, 7, 220-226.

12. Lewin, K. and Grabbe, P. Conduct, Knowledge, and Acceptance of New Values. *Journal of Social Issues*, 1945, 56-64.

4. the cursillo

The cursillo retreat movement has been responsible for popularizing a more active format for retreats. The cursillo may not have been the first to introduce informal group singing, written and artistic expression, group discussions, and similar activities; but the movement has been clearly identified as the first significant attempt to utilize these techniques in order to bring more meaning to the period of retreat. Not enough can be said for the value of the cursillo movement as an innovation and its courage in breaking sharply from tradition previously unchallenged.

The ability of the cursillo to affect large numbers of people cannot be described in other than spectacular terms. The many years of experience attached to the traditional retreat, the lack of interest in novel methods, and a considerable amount of inertia were formidable obstacles to overcome. When one further realizes that a psychological resistance to change was also operating within the Church at the time the cursillo gained its initial popularity, the dimensions to which the movement has obviously grown are even more incredible.

Lest some misunderstand these statements in their apparent naïveté, it should be pointed out that in many ways the Church was ready for the kind of change which the cursillo proposed. Witness to this fact is the ease with which the Vatican Council precipitated many changes of a similar nature within many other areas of the Church. While it might be suggested by some that the experience of many centuries made change undesirable, others would point to the stagnation which grew through those same centuries making such change a welcome relief. More than a welcome relief, however, many were convinced our knowledge of the related fields of psychology, sociology, etc., was making the lack of change in antiquated methods increasingly ludicrous in the eyes of those both in and out of the Church. These and other factors make it obvious that there were forces within the Church and society that aided the cursillo movement in attaining its immense popularity.

If the movement had gained instant appeal from many sides and then died quickly, we might have suggested that the movement had its basic appeal in the novelty offered to those in the movement. But the cursillo shows little sign of dying. Those within the movement will admit that a plateau might well have been reached; but it is obviously a plateau which continues to draw significant numbers of converts into the cursillo each year. Far from being a novelty which passes like so many fads experienced in life generally, the cursillo has roots which are much deeper and more nourishing.

It would be self-deceiving to hide from the real contribution of the cursillo to the religious life of its followers. The testimony of persons who have found a new meaning in their religion through the cursillo make it impossible to deny the fact that there is value implicit in this retreat activity for a large number of persons. One must recognize from this evidence that something within the format reaches many persons at a more fundamental level than previously experienced. This is all the more significant when one discovers some of these same people speak of their previous religious activity as being little more than routine and legalistic.

Objections will be raised later to some of the techniques used by the cursillo; but it should be made clear now that they are made in the context of a strong positive feeling for the cursillo generally. In this context, not enough can be said about the positive value the cursillo has had in breaking old stereotypes concerning the manner in which the retreat should be conducted. One of the biggest obstacles to making the retreat experience meaningful to more people was the feeling that the retreat had to be done a certain predetermined way. Encompassed within this feeling was an undefined fear that if the retreat were not carried out in a certain manner, the entire experience would somehow be invalid.

Later thoughts will suggest that much more of the dynamic could be unleashed than the cursillo now allows in its highly structured format, but full credit should be given to the movement for breaking down much of the resistance to introducing group discussion into the retreat period. It is felt that part of the great success resulting from cursillo experiences may be attributed to the fact that some of the dynamic potential in group experiences is unleashed in the cursillo retreat. Though such experiences, by their very nature, must be uneven in their results, there is every indication that normally those making the cursillo — the cursillistas — do experience the positive dynamic that one always attempts to unleash in a group experience. One hears of the positive affection developed between those making the cursillo together, many witness to the openness which develops during the weekend, and previous barriers to understanding the person of Christ in others seem to have been overcome. All of this very strongly suggests that a genuine and positive dynamic operates between those making the cursillo.

Without any doubt, other cursillo techniques contribute to the release of this dynamic which has so many positive effects upon those participating in the weekend. The informal folk song sessions, the expression in art and writing, the participation at Mass, and other activities of the weekend blend together to create a cohesion with the group which is most conducive to expression of Christian love. Of course, some attempts are not as effective as others in reaching the desired goal and some experiences are not as genuine as others in their total impact; but many are drawn much closer to Christ and his message by means of the cursillo retreat in its present form.

Imitations of the cursillo now being employed further prove that the results are inspiring. The Better World retreats and the Study Weekends now popular on college campuses seem to have originated in the basic cursillo format. These adaptations may result from an attempt to improve on the "original product" and, therefore, implicitly find weaknesses in its structure; but this does not negate the fact that the cursillo is the pattern from which all develop. Like all originals, the cursillo will be much abused because of the very fact that it is the first form of new retreat in many centuries. Improvements will often be made on the basic format because of failures on the part of those attempting to be successful in its application.

While there is much to be said in favor of the cursillo, there are, on the other hand, things about it which may be harmful. Whenever man attempts to structure any experience which is fundamentally human, he must constantly be careful so that he does not allow his attention to dwell principally upon the structure rather than on the human beings he is placing within the structure. The human aspects of life are unpredictable by their very nature and the subtle temptation is to turn our attention to the structure of the event which is so much more easily controlled. If we turn our attention to how much time should be spent in the group discussion during the cursillo, for example, we do not have to face the anxiety and frustration of the more fundamental question which asks whether or not that discussion will have any meaning. In the case of experiential failure, it is also much easier to escape behind the rationalization that it was the structure which broke down rather than admit that those attempting to "stage" the event had little interest in or understanding of the human persons who create an experience in the context of a structure.

A sure sign that a person or an institution has reached maturity is the ease with which criticisms are handled. When the criticisms grow to the proportion of blanket condemnations, therefore, there is clear indication that a movement has stabilized its uneven growth and will not be unhinged by the frantic voice of a few. In order to properly assess the criticisms the cursillo is receiving in its maturity, one must look, first of all, to the source of the criticisms. From the person who is constantly harassed to make the cursillo by his well-intentioned friends, to the retreat master of thirty years' experience who recognizes the cursillo as a threat to his lifework, one might discover the very same charge. Obviously, however, the validity of their criticisms may be poles apart.

The cursillo has reached a significant degree of recognition within the Church and there is no doubt that it is now a valid topic for criticism. There is no desire to criticize the cursillo out of the positive context cited earlier in this chapter; but the structure of this form of retreat deserves to be examined a little more closely. From such a criticism, the positive movement already effected by the cursillo in making the retreat a more meaningful experience will perhaps gather the momentum which can be a positive force in the Church. The criticism will be harsh and many will undoubtedly say unfounded. If there is no foundation to the criticism, there would then be no reason to expect such criticism to take roots in the reflection of others.

We often hear the cursillo described as a "brainwashing" session by those seriously opposed to it. Whether they have heard others use the term or have personally examined the actual experience and found an analogy with "brainwashing" tactics, they are clear in their reference and do not normally qualify the use of the term. There is little doubt about the emotional level of a discussion in this context.

Many would find fault with even beginning to compare the cursillo retreat to "brainwashing" in any form; but it will be attempted here in order to discover whether or not there is any validity to the often articulated charge. It would seem that if the charge is as ludicrous as some seem to suggest, an honest examination of any genuine comparisons would immediately point out that fact. If, on the other hand, analogies are present, such an examination would put them in their proper context outside the blanket condemnation which the term "brainwashing" implies.

The true context of the term "brainwashing" in its most emotional context can best be seen in its original form. The term originated as a description of the Chinese indoctrination program for the prisoners of war and most of the genuinely negative overtones arise from its reference to the experiences of United Nations prisoners of war in the hands of the Chinese

Communists during the Korean conflict. Referring to the cursillo as an attempt at "brainwashing" evokes the negative feelings most of us have toward that ugly period of recent history.
It is only by making the comparison to the cursillo in this context that we face up to the true dimensions of the charge.

In order to properly understand the indoctrination program
used by the Chinese Communists in Korea, we must first of all
clear away some of the vague notions many have toward the
process and its effectiveness. Following the repatriation of United
Nations prisoners of war in August, 1953,

> a rash of testimonial articles appeared in weekly magazines,
> some attempting to show that the Chinese Communist tech-
> niques were so terrifying that no one could withstand them,
> others roundly condemning the collaborative activities of the
> so-called "progressives" as having been selfishly motivated
> under conditions in which resistance was possible. These
> various accounts fall short because they are too emotionally
> charged to be objective, and, because they fail to have any
> generality, since they are usually based on the personal ex-
> periences of only one man.[1]

Enough time has passed for us to understand the actual tactics
of the Chinese Communists, but many are still confused as to
the exact dimensions of the indoctrination technique used in
Korea. In order to gain proper perspective on the entire program, we must find a more objective standpoint from which to
view the Korean "brainwashing" than individual accounts or
vague personal recollections.

One of the best studies done on the Chinese indoctrination
program is an article[2] written by Edgar H. Schein and published
in the journal *Psychiatry*. Schein based his article on the experiences of several randomly selected men, thus escaping the
subjectivity which surrounded the entire subject during that
time.

> Of approximately 20 repatriates selected at random at dif-
> ferent stages of the repatriation, each was asked to tell in
> chronological order and in as great detail as possible what

had happened to him during his captivity. Emphasis was placed on what the Chinese or North Koreans *did* in their handling of the prisoners and how the men reacted. Then men were particularly encouraged to relate the reactions of *others,* in order to avoid arousing anxiety or guilt over their own behavior and thereby blocking the flow of memories.[3]

In order to best understand the process of "brainwashing" attempted by the Chinese, one should place it in its proper context. Initial emphasis will be placed upon the atmosphere which was present as a result of the captor's attitude and the environmental conditions which prevailed. The Chinese attitude toward the prisoners lay between the extremes of friendliness and hostility. The prevailing attitude was an apparent friendliness, but a threat of death always remained over the head of the individual who did not conform.

> The Chinese . . . often tried to create an atmosphere of friendliness and leniency. Some men reported that their Chinese captors approached them with outstretched hands, saying, "Congratulations! You've been liberated." It was made clear to the man that he could now join forces with other "fighters for peace." This Chinese tactic was part of their *"lenient-policy,"* which was explained to groups of prisoners shortly after capture in these terms: Because the UN had entered the war illegally and was an aggressor, all UN military personnel were in fact "war criminals" and could be shot summarily. But the average soldier was, after all, only carrying out orders for his leaders who were the real criminals. Therefore, the Chinese would consider the POW a "student" and would teach him the "truth" about the war. Anyone who did not cooperate by going to school and by learning voluntarily could be reverted to his "war-criminal" status and shot, particularly if a confession could be obtained from him.[4]

Though none of the many Communists' threats which hung over the heads of the POW in Korea prevail in the cursillo, something of the atmosphere can be transferred by analogy to the retreat weekend. An atmosphere of "friendly persuasion" does dominate many cursillo weekends. Beginning with those who "choose" the participant to enjoy the weekend and continuing through the retreat itself, the individual experience is geared to make the retreatant feel he is a "student" about to learn the "truth" concerning his religion. This attitude may be much more subtle than that prevailing in a prison camp, but the pressure to conform to opinions expressed might very well be more intense. There is no hint that the freedom experienced by the cursillo retreatant is blocked in the same manner or to the same degree as that of the POW. Still the analogy does point up the fact that some pressure to conform exists during the weekend. Experiences will vary from one retreat to another, but the pressure to conform, in all forms, amounts to a fundamental lack of freedom.

Poor food, lack of sleep, inadequate medical supplies, and presence of disease made Korean prisoners ill-prepared physically and psychologically for the indoctrination pressures they were about to face. While the initial attempt to compare the poor physical condition of the prisoners to that of the retreatants appears ludicrous at first glance, the analogy is not entirely without its significance. The effects of a fast-paced day and a maximum of six hours' sleep at night tend to break down the physical endurance of even the healthiest person. This breakdown of psychological resistance would not begin to reach the intense level experienced by the prisoners in Korea, yet the structure of the cursillo lends itself to lowering the individual's resistance to any form of indoctrination. Again we sense something of an analogy between the techniques used in Korea and those used in the cursillo. The techniques discovered in the cursillo are analogous enough to make the term "brainwashing" not altogether inaccurate.

Most people rely on the opinion of others to determine whether they are "right" or "wrong" in their judgments. An important goal of the Communists in their attempt to indoctrinate the prisoner, therefore, was to isolate him socially. All sources of information from the outside world were cut off save carefully selected propaganda journals which supported the heavy bias of the Communists. Even mail delivery was systematically manipulated to allow only letters containing no general information or bad personal news through to the prisoner. Finally, in order to further break down any internal structure in groups which might be formed, men were segregated according to rank.

Determined efforts to undermine any friendships, emotional bonds, or group activities, further structured the isolation of one man from any outside evaluation of his judgments. The systematic use of spies within the ranks was effective in making everyone fearful of placing confidence in others. From such a general feeling of distrust, the only safe course appeared to be to withdraw from intimate interaction with other prisoners.

> From the point of view of this analysis, the most important effect of the social isolation which existed was the consequent emotional isolation which prevented a man from validating any of his beliefs, attitudes, and values through meaningful interaction with other men at a time when these were under heavy attack from many sources and when no accurate information was available.[5]

The suggestion that the effects of the cursillo could create something of the same social isolation experienced by the prisoners in Korea might be startling. This is especially true in view of the fact that thousands of cursillistas will attest to the greater degree of insight they gained as a result of the cursillo experience. These retreatants will claim to have never before been so close to others as a result of such relatively short exposure. With so much evidence to oppose such a view, how could anyone suggest that the cursillo isolates one person from another?

If one is to gain proper perspective on the issue, he must look at the structure of the weekend before discussing its ramifications. The fact is that the cursillo is a highly structured series of activities which allows little to no time for the personal kind of discussion in which one might reveal his reactions to what is being discussed and any possible doubts about the validity of particular statements. Without the time to sort out such reactions with others, one has lost a primary source of validating his reaction. With this prop removed, people tend to more readily accept whatever they are told is true, which is another way of saying they are more susceptible to "brainwashing."

There is, in fact, no incompatibility between being close to someone and not knowing his reactions to a given statement or issue. There is every reason to believe that the dynamic released within the cursillo draws persons closer together, but this does not imply that they necessarily have had the leisure to understand each other's position on what is constantly being expressed as the theme of the occasion which drew them together. Much of the confusion caused by this unusual distinction will be clarified when we consider the rest of the framework in which the personal bond between cursillistas develops.

Under normal circumstances, there are five talks given every day of the cursillo lasting approximately one hour each. Some of the talks may be given by priests or other religious, but normally the majority are given by laymen from all walks of life. Though some latitude is allowed for personal style or taste, these talks are carefully outlined as to their content. Since fifteen hours of the three-day period are given over to these talks, one would have to conclude that these talks form the cornerstone upon which the retreat is built. The possible effect such talks can have on individuals might be better understood if we look at the use of lectures by the Chinese Communists to indoctrinate United Nations soldiers.

> The chief method of direct indoctrination was a series of lectures that all prisoners had to attend at some time during their imprisonment. These lectures were given daily and lasted from two to three hours. Each camp had one or more political instructors who read the lectures from a prepared text. . . . The constant hammering at certain points, combined with all the other techniques used — and in a situation where the prisoners had no access to other information — made it likely that many of the Chinese arguments did filter through enough to make many of the men question some of

their former points of view. . . . Perhaps the most effective attack on existing values, beliefs, and attitudes was the use of testimonials from prisoners who were ostensibly supporting Communist enterprises. These included peace petitions, radio appeals, speeches, and confessions. The use of such testimonials had a double effect in that it further weakened group ties while presenting pro-Communist arguments. As long as the men unanimously rejected the propaganda, each of them could firmly hold to the position that his beliefs must be right, even if he could not defend them logically. However, *if even one other man became convinced, it was no longer possible to hold this position.* Each man was then required to begin examining his beliefs and was vulnerable to the highly one-sided arguments that were repeatedly presented.[6]

A great similarity with the indoctrination program in Korea emerges when we consider the talks of the cursillo. Though obvious distinctions could be drawn, the fact is that a great deal of a man's day, in either case, is given over to talks which follow a determined pattern. Spending a great deal of time hearing talks which follow closely a given train of thought will lower a man's resistance to the ideas expressed and make him susceptible to indoctrination. Whether the "brainwashing" which emerges is intentional or not, is effective or not, has positive effects or not, is really not brought into question here. What we are attempting to determine is whether the sum total effect of whatever happens during the cursillo weekend is a form of indoctrination. It is felt that no apology is necessary for the fact that we are not considering motives in this analysis. Persons with the very best motives in the world can be indoctrinating others without any consciousness of the fact. This does not mean that their indoctrination is any less manipulative.

In the direct attacks which I have been discussing, the source of propaganda was external. In the indirect attacks, a set of conditions was created in which each prisoner of war was encouraged to participate in a way that would make it more possible for him to accept some of the new points of view. One attempt to accomplish this was by means of group discussions following lectures. Most lectures ended with a series of conclusions — for example, "The South Koreans started the war by invading North Korea," or "The aim of the capitalist nations is world domination." The men were then required to break up into squads, go to their quarters, and discuss the material for periods of two hours or more. At the end of the discussion each squad had to provide written answers to questions handed out during the lecture — the answers, obviously, which had already been provided in the lecture. To "discuss" the lecture thus meant, in effect, to rationalize the predetermined conclusions.[7]

As we examine this area more closely, we see a greater and greater analogy between the cursillo and the techniques used by the Chinese Communists. The cursillo gathers the audience together in small groups for the purpose of discussing the points made in the talks. The purpose of the discussion is directed along the same lines though the questions may be somewhat more subtly stated in the cursillo. But despite the striking similarity of the lecture-discussion in the general outline, there is one rather sharp distinction to be drawn.

In contrast to the discussions used by the Communists which would last for two hours or more, the parallel discussions following the lectures in the cursillo normally last somewhere between ten and twenty minutes. The Communists were obviously striving for maximum effectiveness in their "brainwashing" tactics when they extended the discussions to two hours or more, but this says nothing about the effectiveness of short discussions in accomplishing the same goal of indoctrination. Viewed in a certain light, it could readily be claimed that the short discussion might be more effective in orienting participants along any given line of reasoning.

The person in the cursillo who listens to a point being made for about an hour before being allowed to discuss it briefly will probably not have enough time in discussion to intelligently evaluate the truth of any conclusion drawn. It would seem reasonable to expect little more than a succinct restatement of the talk to emerge in the few minutes' discussion available to the members of the group. There certainly would not be enough time available for someone who objected to a conclusion reached by the lecturer to clearly establish his opinion. If an opinion is expressed which is clearly at odds with the conclusion expected by the team giving the retreat, the team members move quickly in their attempts to return the deviate to the fold.

One of the social pressures which is most effective in creating conformity on the part of the errant participant is the use of the term "holdout" when referring to him. As the group begins to adopt this term in referring to the cursillista who does not accept some part of the doctrine which has been a major conclusion of any given talk, an enormous degree of internal pressure builds which is most effective in helping the "holdout" begin to accept the conclusion of the majority.

Another effective means of creating consensus in the cursillo is closely paralleled by the methods used in Korea. In order to assure the team that group discussions do not stray too far from the conclusions reached in the talk, each group is provided with a "plant" who is normally thought to be making the cursillo for the first time by the others in the group. With the "plant" present in the group to stimulate and guide discussion along certain lines predetermined by the team, there is even less chance that objections may arise from group members. Employment of such techniques as the short discussion period, in contrast to the long talks, and the presence of the "plant" whose function is to guide the group along certain predetermined lines, might easily result in a consensus reached through indoctrination.

A monitor was assigned to each squad to "aid" the men in the discussion, to make sure that they stayed on the proper topic, and to collect the answers and make sure that they were the "right" ones. Initially, the monitor for most squads was an English-speaking Chinese, but whenever possible the Chinese turned the job over to one of the squad members, usually the one who was most cooperative or sympathetic to the Communist point of view. If one or more members of the squad turned in "wrong" answers — for example, saying that the North Koreans had invaded South Korea — the entire squad had to listen to the lecture again and repeat the group discussion.[8]

No such overt pressure as repeating the discussion until the correct answer emerges exists in the cursillo, but there is no doubt in the minds of the team giving the retreat that there is indeed a correct conclusion to be drawn by the group. If any given group consistently arrived at a conclusion which was not the same one predetermined by the team, the discussion would be considered a failure. There appears to be no better definition of indoctrination than the concerted effort to create an atmosphere most conducive to precipitating predeterminated conclusions from an individual or group.

At one point in Schein's article on "brainwashing," he summarizes the general principles which the Communists applied to all techniques of indoctrination. There is again no exact parallel with the cursillo, but a parallel does exist and some of the general principles may be applied to the cursillo as validly as they can to the Communist methods in Korea. The cursillo application differs from the Communist application basically in intensity rather than in any essential difference in the principle itself.

> Several general principles underlay the various phases of the Chinese indoctrination, which may be worth summing up at this point. The first of these was *repetition*. One of the chief characteristics of the Chinese was their immense patience in whatever they were doing; whether they were conducting an interrogation, giving a lecture, chiding a prisoner, or trying to obtain a confession, they were always willing to make their demand or assertion over and over again. Many men pointed out that most of the techniques used gained their effectiveness by being used in this repetitive way until the prisoner could no longer sustain his resistance.[9]

There is clearly a difference between the intensity of the repetition described above and that present in the cursillo. But to conclude, therefore, that there is no parallel would be to ignore the obvious use of repetition in the cursillo. By repeating the central themes over and over in the talks and discussions by making these same themes the subject of written and oral expression, by focusing on the themes informally, the cursillo is obviously using repetition to reduce resistance in the cursillistas. To ignore this fact is to ignore the atmosphere which the cursillo is structured to create.

> A second characteristic was the *pacing of demands*. In the various kinds of responses that were demanded of the prisoners, the Chinese always started with trivial, innocuous one and, as the habit of responding became established, gradually worked up to more important ones. Thus after a prisoner had once been "trained" to speak or write out trivia, statements on more important issues were demanded of him. This was particularly effective in eliciting confessions, self-criticism, and information during interrogation.[10]

If anyone were to question the methods of the cursillo because it paced its demands on the participants, the obvious reply would be to request an alternate method. A teacher must begin with easy concepts and work to the more difficult. It is unreasonable to suggest another approach. The fact still remains that, given the structure of the cursillo generally, the pacing of demands further reduces any cursillista's ability to resist indoctrination.

> Closely connected with the principle of pacing was the principle of constant *participation* from the prisoner. It was never enough for the prisoner to listen and absorb; some kind of verbal or written response was always demanded. Thus, if a man would not give original material in question-and-answer sessions, he was asked to copy something. Likewise, group discussions, autobiographical statements, self-criticisms, and public confessions all demanded an active participation by the prisoner.[11]

The reason for including participation is apparently quite

different from the motives of the Communists, but there is again no doubt that the individual cursillista more readily accepts group conclusions because he actively participates. The cursillistas are expected to participate in a number of different ways during the course of the weekend. Over and above listening to lectures and participating in group discussions, the retreatant writes, sings, and draws pictures in ways designed to reinforce the conclusions expected from the team which structures the weekend.

The parallels between the indoctrination used in Korea and that used by the cursillo show that the use of the term "brainwashing" to describe the weekend is not completely inaccurate. One would be safe in saying that the cursillo "brainwashes" its participants if he understood that the term is only applied by analogy. The analogy does fit in the ways just described; however, it is also important to qualify it in order that the term be used in its proper context.

There are even more obvious distinctions to be drawn between the cursillo and the tactics used by the Communists. The lack of decent living conditions, medical supplies, food, and sanitary conditions, the pressures to conform, including the ultimate threat of execution, the long and tedious interrogations, the overt rewards of better living conditions and supplies offered to those who would cooperate with Communist "peace" attempts, have little or no counterpart in the cursillo. The more obvious extremes used in Korea are simply not a part of the retreat weekend.

There is still a question as to whether or not the very fact that the Communists' pressures were overt made them less effective in the indoctrination program. If it is true that the pressures toward conformity which are found in the cursillo are essentially the same, the very fact of their subtle nature might make them even more effective in indoctrinating the participants in certain value systems. Though we do not yet have a scientific manner of measuring the difference between the two types of indoctrination, there are valid reasons to speculate that

the more subtle forms of indoctrination found in the cursillo
may be the most effective.

It might be that because of the overtones the word "brainwashing" has for the vast majority of people it would be directly
misleading in connection with the cursillo. But there are ample
parallels to justify applying the essential meaning of the word
without the emotional context which necessarily arises with the
use of the term. The actual use of the term with all its emotional overtones, however, would seem unjustified.

Implicit in most of the discussion thus far has been the
assumption that indoctrination is something undesirable and
most people would agree to this. However, we would find on
close examination that they do not object to indoctrination when
the goals of such manipulation are seen as desirable. In classical
terms applied to this instance, there are those who will accept
indoctrination as justifiable in view of a desirable end.

In the realm of religion and religious thought, many get
confused concerning what is and is not desirable. While they
would not want it said that they approved of indoctrination on
any level, their notion of the "absolute truth" of the Church
makes them wonder if indoctrination is not justified under certain circumstances. If we could say that certain truths are
absolute and accepting them is a movement toward man's understanding of his relationship to God, then any method used
to convince man of these truths could and should be used.

If we understand the truth of the Church as a package of
facts wrapped in a covering of particular terminology and neatly
tied with a ribbon of syllogistic logic, there might be some justification for pressuring people to accept such a means to natural
and supernatural happiness. But if we understand the truth
of the Church as something man must constantly reexamine
in the light of new discoveries in science, sociology, psychology,
and other academic disciplines, constantly restate in terminology compatible with such discoveries, and constantly evaluate
in the light of theological evolution, then the application of
indoctrination techniques seems particularly distasteful.

When we begin to understand religious truth as something which remains stable in its essence as well as evolutionary in its expression, we will also be cautious of any attempts at indoctrination. If man had been satisfied at any point in history with religious truth as it was then expressed, we could not have been able to attain the purified concepts which prevail today. Because Augustine, Aquinas, and other intellectual giants were allowed to exercise their imagination and intelligence in considering religious truth, we have inherited a wealth of insight into the nature of God and man's relation to him.

Each man has a unique relationship with God. He must explore the meaning and depths of this relationship. If the time of retreat is to be valuable for achieving its proper end, it would seem that anything which frustrates free expression should be avoided at all costs. Methods which result in indoctrination of any form clearly frustrate a valuable opportunity for man to further understand his relation to God and move with certainty toward his natural and supernatural end.

The general focus of this chapter concentrated on the comparison between the cursillo techniques and the "brainwashing" tactics used in Korea. The reader might therefore conclude that the author is diametrically opposed to everything the cursillo represents. In order to present a more balanced view, let me reemphasize some of the points made in the beginning of this chapter.

It has been largely from the efforts of the cursillo movement that the concept of the active retreat has become a reality in the life of the Church. And in clearly demonstrating the discontent with the traditional retreat method now present within the Church, the cursillo deserves nothing but praise. The untold numbers of cursillistas ready, willing, and able to attest to the renewal they personally experienced in their spirituality as a result of the weekend experience are a further demonstration of the importance of the cursillo. There simply can be no doubt that these people have found new meaning in their religion through the cursillo in its present form. The success of the cursillo is a fact. One who would deny it would be denying reality.

The aim here is not to deny the success and importance of that success, but to point out that the cursillo is a starting point. From an analysis of the cursillo as it is now structured, it is felt that it lacks a great deal. It is only hoped that the weaknesses in the present structure will be honestly faced with a view toward correction.

REFERENCES

1. Schein, Edgar H. The Chinese Indoctrination Program for Prisoners of War: A Study of Attempted "Brainwashing." In Eleanor E. Maccoby, Theodore M. Newcomb, & Eugene L. Hartley, *Readings in Social Psychology*. New York: Holt, Rinehart and Winston, Inc., 1958, p. 311.
2. Ibid., p. 311-334.
3. Ibid., p. 311.
4. Ibid., p. 312.
5. Ibid., p. 317.
6. Ibid., p. 317-8.
7. Ibid., p. 319.
8. Ibid., p. 319.
9. Ibid., p. 325.
10. Ibid., p. 325.
11. Ibid., p. 325-6.

5. retreat spirituality

Before moving further into a discussion of the value group dynamics may have within a retreat format, we had better face the most fundamental question which can be posed concerning this innovation. The one question which strikes at the heart of the matter is whether or not such group discussions really increase the religious dimension of the retreat experience. If it is possible to answer this question affirmatively, the major obstacle to include dynamics in the retreat will have been removed.

In the years immediately following the Council there has been concern that religion is losing ground and being replaced by secular attitudes. Wherever man appears to dominate an area previously considered sacred, many become disturbed at the possibility that religion will ultimately lose its significance. The introduction of an activity considered basically "psychological" into an area reserved for the "spiritual" may not be a major consideration in itself, but it becomes significant if viewed as part of a movement toward the total secularization of religion.

The apparent humanizing of religion which is taking place is becoming more and more a matter of concern for those within the Christian community and consideration should be given to this problem. Though the concern is becoming widespread enough to include churchmen of all faiths, little or nothing has been written in an attempt to allay fears or create a positive approach to the problem. Little more than a personal reflection on the question can be presented here with the major work to be accomplished in the future.

Today, on every side, inside and outside of theology, we have begun to decide on the critical importance of the order of the secular. The secular order has become a critical Christian interest and concern. Since this is most certainly a fact and since the fact is causing a good deal of theological anxiety, it seems good that we should call the whole question central and should devote a good deal of time and energy to it over the next generation.[1]

When the average Christian of good faith considers the human in contrast to the sacred, he normally labors under misconceptions of the vast difference between the two. Considered in a certain light, the human cannot be compared to the sacred by any but the weakest kind of analogy. Yet if one reflects on the meaning of the phrase "grace builds on nature," he discovers there is no other way for him to describe the true meaning of the sacred except by means of this admittedly weak analogy.

The human suffers from a false evaluation in the minds of many Christians. No doubt such negative values were instilled by persons whose goal was to elevate the religious dimension of man's existence, but often the human and secular loses its proper significance in the minds of those who most need to properly understand the human to attain both spiritual and human fulfillment. In order to restore human nature to its proper place in the total life experience of the Christian, we must reexamine the meaning Christ gave to the human by his incarnation.

While there are always many ready to stand in the way of any examination of human nature which might appear to change the meaning of the sacred, the need for new definitions becomes more apparent from any honest consideration of the Church in the modern world. If we look at the definition of what the objector considers sacred, Christianity is fighting a losing battle. What has been classically considered sacred is losing ground to the human. The amount of time, energy, and effort man places in the human endeavors of this world is constantly increasing to the apparent detriment of the sacred. Either the Christian must reevaluate his norms for the Christian life or he will increasingly find a need to yield to the inevitable death of the "religious."

> What we might call the sacred or the sacral seems to be in a losing battle. The range of this thing we have been calling the sacred or the holy, the range of religion, the range of theology, the range of Christianity, the range of the symbols of Christianity, seems to be receding more and more at the same time that the life, the activity, the creativity of the secular world take over ever-increasing areas of our consciousness. This, unfortunately, has been a basic image.[2]

In order to establish this consideration on a more optimistic foundation from the very beginning, the development of the human will be considered a goal of Christianity. The pessimist might readily see the human developing only at the expense of a religious decline, but the feeling is that the heart of the Christian message looks to the complete human emergence as its omega point. There appears to be no more logical conclusion to the development of religious thought and effort than the emergence of man in a complete human response to Christ and his message.

Some theologians are all too willing to point to the apparent discrepancies between static theological concepts and the human person emerging within the modern framework. Rather than using theology as an obstacle to the growth potential in man, the need today is for a theology which develops with men in the light of the new consciousness he is experiencing. New directions must be explored in order to maintain significance for theological thought in the future. Rather than see theology lose relevance in a changing world, many are pleading for a witness who will direct and encourage expansion of human nature which they observe as part of their world.

Viewed in the context of a Teilhardian evolutionary process, man is reaching another turning point in the consciousness of himself. As man approaches this complete self-awareness, he will be moving toward the omega point of history which is the ultimate goal of the Christian message. There was a time when man's ultimate consciousness directed him to master and then classify the material things which surround him; he must now begin to move toward God through himself rather than through domination of the material order.

We might focus our attention on the fact of the human emergence and fail to see the emergence of the material order, but it will be just as important in our consideration for us to appreciate the parallel emergence of the secular. We must combine our efforts with those who strive toward the emergence of things material. The very work of the Christian must be to direct this emergence of things material, which he is all too willing to fear and question, in order to see all things renewed in Christ.

It is apparent to the most casual observer that an explosion of the material order is in process. An awareness of the knowledge explosion, the communication explosion, the transportation explosion, and other similar escalations might give man reason to fear that the human dimension of life may be threatened. We have not discovered how to allow man his central position in a world measured with scales previously unknown.

In order to cope with the massive consequences of the emergence of things material, it is important to leave the comfort of passive fear and confront this new world aggressively. We must be a part of this new movement so that we may have a positive influence on its direction, rather than looking upon it as a sacrificing of the sacred. If anything is important in a period when man has lost the guidelines necessary to direct the material universe, it is to have persons internally related to such work who are dedicated to discovering the Christian ramifications implicit in this vast emergence.

> Thus we quickly discover and designate another attitude that Christianity must take toward the emergence of the secular order as secular. It has already occurred to us that we should regard it as a goal rather than a problem, and that our attitude toward it should, therefore, be positive. Now the thought occurs that we should stay on the offensive within this new

situation. We should change our images of our situation. We should stop imagining ourselves, the representatives of a theological and sacral order, as slowly being pushed into an irrelevant corner, into less and less space, by an emerging giant that threatens to take over more and more of the landscape. We must conceive of ourselves as an offensive force that compels and teaches the secular to become itself and to become creative. It needs an outside force to make it become itself. Indeed this will be part of the dialectic I will use in this paper, a dialectic according to which an outside force is needed if we are to have an interior that is free. And in the present case we are in the presence of a giant who tends to be fat and sloppy and to rest on the glory of past accomplishments, who is overly interested in big lines and is having as much trouble as an institution in letting things emerge.[3]

Perhaps the move from this to a consideration of the retreat format may seem a little abrupt and apparently unconnected at first. It is hoped that a consideration of the concrete will be an aid in understanding the ramification implicit in the discussion thus far. Since we are in the midst of the change and cannot hope to see with any clarity the end in view, a reconsideration of the distinction between the material and sacred will be necessary in order to find the proper path toward our goal. There will be little excuse necessary for not clearly seeing the goal at the end of the path if the need to be on this particular path evolves with some clarity.

The assumption is that the retreat format as traditionally considered is a good example of an attempt to give a religious dimension to a human endeavor. If the assumption that the structure represents things sacred in a special manner is valid, it would seem we have a good vantage point from which to consider the actual distinction between the religious and secular.

The first disconcerting element which immediately strikes one reflecting on the traditional concept of the retreat is the manner in which many persons are subjected to exactly the same retreat with little or no regard for the distinction between them as persons. When the traditional talks or sermons are given as an integral part of the retreat, there is little about the exercise which acknowledges whether there are one, twenty, or a hundred persons present.

In its attempt to form a unity in faith from a diversity of persons, the retreat was a genuine attempt to reach a realistic and desirable goal. From the very meaning of the word "catholic," we know that an essential goal of the Faith is to attain an essential unity in our belief. However, if the effort to attain unity is so strong that it destroys the spontaneous diversity, then the evidence clearly indicates a sense of balance has been lost.

The retreat was effective in its methods and served well in helping us move toward our goal of attaining on faith for many people. Like all methods, however, there were good and bad sides to it. Until this point in history we have been all too willing to emphasize only the positive accomplishments of the retreat and either minimize or overlook the very real and often negative aspects.

If we are to clearly understand the mentality which allowed the present condition to develop within the Church, we must consider honestly what sort of growth frustration was permitted to endure beforehand. Certainly there were many manifestations of diversity destruction in order to forge unity within the Church. The retreat is merely one example of this tendency to suppress individuality and is not unlike many similar rites and rituals which have the same overall effect.

When the individual enters the context of a classical retreat, he is asked to shield others from his individual tastes in art and music, from his personal idiosyncrasies, from his unique human and spiritual experiences, and all other manifestations of personality which might create some diversity within the context of the group. By joining all the other retreatants in an effort to create a group which is essentially without individuality, the stage is set to spoon-feed a set of doctrines or dogmas which will be accepted without question or clarification. With the stage thus set for indoctrination techniques, there is little doubt that manipulation will follow whether it is intended or not.

The retreat is a good example of the kind of destructiveness which results from an attempt to create unity, but it is only indicative of the general tone set within the Church. We are gradually becoming more permissive and hopefully beginning to attain the goal of stimulative diversity in all things and all persons. Our immediate concern must naturally be to allow and hopefully stimulate diversity within the context of those things considered sacred, but the ultimate goal should be to encourage the maximum diversity in the secular order.

Attempts to unify at the expense of diversity in the communal prayer life of the Church are readily recognizable. In the liturgical and nonliturgical rites of the Church, as well as in retreats, little individual expression has been allowed. Occasionally, moments of silent prayer were permitted within the context of Church services, but the normal pattern was to restrict communal prayer to set formulas. With such constancy of prayer patterns, it is difficult to imagine that much aid or stimulation was given to the individual in his effort to lift his heart and mind to God.

Part of the success of the dynamic retreat depends upon the ability of the retreat master to create an atmosphere conducive to individual expression in spontaneous prayer. While nothing would be more destructive than coercion to pray before others, an occasion which would allow individuals to offer prayer in the presence of a group can create a sense of Christian community more quickly than any other known expression. Paradoxically, allowing for individual expression precipitates a union between members of a group more effectively than other forms of communal expression.

The rite and ritual of religion have in the past consciously or unconsciously tended to suppress diversity. If we are to take advantage of the full potential of the religious experience, we must begin not only to permit but stimulate diversity in our religious expression. More than giving us an insight into the further dimension which religion may offer generally, the consideration of the retreat also suggests the approach which would be most conducive to evolving a spirit of Christianity in the secular world generally.

If we return to our consideration of the material world, we

recall that the mark of our times is the simultaneous emergence of persons and things. When faith in the creative process is at its peak, man considers this emergence as a tendency of all things to assert their identity. If the creative process is considered operative, Christians would adopt the state of mind which not only allows but even encourages this emergence of the material and secular world.

Taking one more logical step into the argument we see the holy as the composite of forces which compel the world to seek its individual identity. When the individual is able to sort out this concept for himself, he begins to see the connection between the material and spiritual worlds. No longer will he need to experience a split personality in an attempt to live in two worlds simultaneously, but rather he will see the sacred or holy impinging directly upon the material. In fact, the holy will only be considered present when related directly to the emergence of the personal world.

> By secular, then it is beginning to be clear to me, as I work through this argument, that I mean a spirit of mind which allows things to emerge on their own terms and a state of reality in which this is or should be going on, this state of emerging, this standing of things on their own identities. This, at any rate, is or would be the ideal state of the secular, the state toward which it should be pushed even when it is unwilling. We had been using a vocabulary according to the terms of which the secular means (in a very negative sense) that which is not the holy, whereas I am suggesting that we shift our images and our vocabulary, that we interpret the secular in terms of emergence and identity and that we conceive of the holy as the force, certainly one of the great forces, which will compel the secular to be itself.[4]

As we focus on the desire within man to emerge and society's tendency to frustrate such emergence, the need for creative effort to permit the quest for identity becomes clearer. With this accent on the most striking relationship between the secular and holy, it is hoped that the Christian may unify these apparently diverse concepts.

We see the emergence of man in his individuality in many striking examples. The civil rights movement which is so much a part of our national scene today gives us a sharp image of man beginning to recognize his own inherent dignity. There are present in society many forces hostile to this movement, as well as the principle represented, yet the very force of the movement at this time demonstrates a new peak in society's recognition of its own dignity.

The forces opposing the civil rights movement may be the most dramatic example of the self-destructive tendency experienced in the Western world, but the very structure upon which most of our society is based is much more telling in its effect. Glancing only superficially at the structure of the industrial giant this country has offered to the world as the goal of democracy, we see the subordinate role man has granted to himself. With his creativity and talents frustrated in the assembly line process, Western man is apparently dedicated to eliminating any tendency for individual emergence.

> A mechanical organization is a completely preplanned, purely rational and logical organization, a pattern for work or life, created and controlled from above, without any participating decision from the subordinates, and which uses only some minimal talent of the human beings caught in the pattern. It does not allow anything but a small fraction of human identity to emerge. It breeds passivity, submissiveness and dependence, all of the wrong kind. In fact it often requires these qualities of human beings, in order to insure its own well-being or profit or development. And the more mature the people involved, the more painful and self-limiting will be their relation to such systems.[5]

With his individuality forced into a mold, man can expect little but a passive dependence upon the system which assures his survival. Society can expect little or nothing from the vast pool of human resources forced into mechanical habits and attitudes. The system produces an ultimate irony as a result of its establishment and it is an even more severe penalty that it imposes upon the mature and creative who are trapped within its confines.

Against this background of frustration to man's individuality and dignity, it requires little thought to suggest the goal for the Christian in the modern world. If Christ's message means anything in contrast to the world which surrounds and restricts man, it means that Christianity must be a force which permits man to emerge as a distinct creation made in the image of God. By his words and actions, Christ preached to all men of all times the ultimate dignity of man and his unique capacity for love. If our society will not allow man's individuality to emerge, then it is reserved to the Christian to witness to the world a readiness to expend ultimate effort in order to precipitate man's emergence.

> I want to be both firm and sober about the way I express this new concept, for we must move thoughtfully wherever we explore an identification between the holy and the secular; indeed I shall suggest later that the very existence of the secular as secular and the emergence of the secular as secular depend in great part upon the parallel emergence of the holy as holy. Granted all that, I repeat that in our discussion we are reaching areas where the holy and the secular are sharing common areas, and where the secular may do a better job of expressing the holy than the older vocabulary and much of the older ascetical vocabulary of the holy.
>
> I am not trying to secularize the holy. That is not the vocabulary I am using. I am saying that the life of the holy often exists with the secular and that in many senses it achieves itself only to the degree that the secular achieves itself.[6]

The retreat format which dominated the scene for many centuries more or less consciously imitated the tendency in man to suppress and restrict any sense of individuality and creativity. By expecting the identical response from each person, the format allowed man to remain as repressed in his response to his religion as he was likely to be toward the world generally. Religion was thus in the unfortunate position of frustrating man's attempts to emerge rather than answering his frustration. Far from witnessing Christ's emphasis on the unique individuality each man has, religion was trapped into supporting the one repressive trend in the world.

If man is to experience his uniqueness in the context of a retreat, he must be afforded the opportunity for genuine participation. It seems obvious that if he is to realize his potential as a creative person capable of a distinct relationship with God, each one must begin to think of this relationship as individual and not identical to every other Christian. For not only will denial of this opportunity to participate tend to negate his sense of worth, but will also pave the way for reactive and restive behavior which is conducive to personal withdrawal from the activity. Men can readily devaluate not only the experience but also the goals such an experience is calculated to instill through this tendency to withdraw.

The retreat, in its worst expression, almost completely denies the opportunity to communicate. When barriers to such communication reach their peak, hostile attitudes between individuals and the retreat master can more readily develop. A sense of free communication, on the other hand, provides the chance to eliminate misunderstanding and conflicts in their early stages.

What is far more important than reducing conflict, however, is that a freedom to communicate allows for a development of understanding between members of a group. Even in an atmosphere where free communication occurs, it is frequently difficult for persons to understand one another. Semantic difficulties alone cause persons to spend a great deal of time clarifying their thoughts. People experience much misunderstanding due to the fact of their individuality even when there is maximum freedom and sincerity. The difficulties present under normal circumstances make one appreciate the almost impossible task of communicating when the atmosphere is overly restrictive.

Many atmospheres restrict freedom of communication by their structure, but the traditional retreat format is undoubtedly one of the most restrictive due to its imposition of silence. Past evaluations of this attempt to create silence never closely examined the negative aspects. By examining the misunderstandings which necessarily occur when freedom to communicate is so drastically limited, it appears one might gain a more balanced structure in the retreat with some revision.

An increase in freedom to communicate would be genuinely desirable, if for no other reason than to aid the retreat master in his ability to know whether or not he is genuinely reaching the retreatants. But far more than the mere ability to speak must be created if one is to encourage free communication in a group. In order for a person to address himself honestly to another, he must feel he is in a "safe" atmosphere. Any indication that what he says will be used by others as a judgment against him will prevent him from revealing himself honestly in his speech. When he feels he is being listened to carefully in an accepting manner, there will be greater effort at honesty and clarity. As persons sense that they will be accepted in their doubt, frustration, and even their hostility, the opportunity for creativity and self-actualization from them will be released so that they may begin to allow themselves to emerge as distinct personalities.

This internal force which allows man to emerge as an individual is the sacred principle discussed earlier. God's creative intent seems clear. By establishing a drive for individuality and personally preaching the sanctity implicit in releasing this drive, he gave to the Christian the unique concept of witness. Since the purpose of our religious rite and ritual is to render the witness intended by Christ, it must release within man a consciousness of his uniqueness and precipitate further appreciation of the diversity necessary in the mature Christian world.

The one argument against the inclusion of group dynamics in retreats which is heard above all others is the charge that such an attempt would be basically geared to making a retreat a form of therapy rather than spirituality. The fundamental fear is that in some way a religious expression is being turned into a psychological experience and will become a regular part of the retreat. It is possible to answer the objection logically, but no discussion will be really adequate to eliminate or even reduce the fear which forms the basis for much of the criticism.

The goals of group dynamics and group therapy are distinct

and separate. The goal of therapy is always to cure psychological aberrations, whereas the goal of the dynamic is to create a free atmosphere in which the individuals are able to explore their thoughts, feelings and experiences more honestly than is possible during their normal daily life. If this goal is clear in the mind of the individual attempting to determine whether or not group dynamics has a place in the retreat format, than he is in a realistic position to objectively explore the role which such activity might play in the experience.

When the dynamic is even partially successful in achieving its goal, the individual participant gains some degree of insight into his true identity. He gains a perspective to look beyond the facades which normally block his vision of himself. The thought of gaining some insight into one's self can be disturbing, but it creates significant fear only for those persons who are generally out of contact with themselves.

One who fears his religious orientation is not basic to his life would have genuine reason to fear the honest soul searching which group dynamics precipitates. Unless religious commitment is very much a part of the person underneath all the facades which he has erected for himself, an honest involvement in such a discussion could be a more fundamental threat than he would be able to risk. Honesty concerning religious orientation can create a richer sense of commitment; it can also pose a genuine fear for one who might suspect superficiality in his religious life.

For the person who has no reason to believe his religious commitment is based on mere externals, the chance to explore himself honestly opens the strong possibility of discovering new depth in his religion. Religion must exist as a part of our true self if it is to have any lasting and valuable effect on our lives. In the normal course of events, we have little opportunity to gain an insight into our personal relationship to religious belief. Only in the "safe and nonthreatening" atmosphere of acceptance can we hope to begin to see what impact religion can and should have in our normal activities. The goal of group dynamics is to allow us to look honestly at the self which we normally tend to hide from ourselves and others. It can be a valuable tool in aiding us to discover and enrich through that discovery the religious reality which lies at the basis of our existence.

The dynamic does more than just allow the participant an insight into his true religious self; it also creates an atmosphere conducive to his emergence. The experience of participating in group dynamic sessions with many divergent ends in view helps us discover a common tendency for the individual to emerge in his true identity. If the goal of the Christian is to witness the necessity of personal emergence in order to fulfill the plan of creation, then the opportunity to do so in the context of a religious retreat is the most significant goal which the retreat experience might accomplish.

Whether one would accent the discovery of the true religious self or the emergence of the individual in an argument for the inclusion of the dynamic in a retreat, it becomes clear that such an inclusion is designed to further the spirituality of the retreatant. The use of group dynamics is a genuine attempt to make the retreat more conducive to increasing the spiritual nature of the format, not an attempt to turn it into a psychological expression. But the dynamic does more than increase the personal spirituality of each participant; it also creates a stronger possibility that the entire group will have a great chance to experience the true meaning of Christian community.

The attempt to include group dynamics in a retreat has often been interpreted as a means of losing a sense of personalism in religion, but a closer examination will demonstrate the dynamic to be one of the best means of developing a genuine personal relationship with Christ and one's neighbor. If we look beyond the individual experience, however, we see that the group phenomenon also gives the person a notion of Christian community in its purest form. Only in the context of a balanced interaction between the sense of personal and collective growth can one realize the true notion of community.

When one genuinely experiences a communal sense in a given group, there is an understanding between members. More than just feeling understood as an individual by others, one gains the ability and desire to take the time and effort to really understand what others are attempting to communicate. A genuine Christlike desire to understand and appreciate others in their unique individuality develops in each person, overcoming the fear of being misunderstood or hurt.

From this honest attempt to understand one another, group members begin to create an atmosphere of acceptance within the community gathered. The acceptance of one another grows, generating a feeling of security, confidence and spontaneity between retreatants. When one begins to sense this freedom within the group, there is a real opportunity to experience Christian charity in a more basic way than is normally available. It would seem that there is no better goal for a retreat than to create such an opportunity for love between fellow Christians.

If the experience is successful in bringing these results into the context of the retreat, each will notice a gradual increase in concern for the group present. One commonly notices in the beginning of most group experiences that the behavior of individuals focuses on their own needs and tensions. If the leader is successful in listening carefully to these egocentric concerns and conveys understanding toward the individuals expressing them, people are freed to look beynd their own needs and become concerned with the needs of others. Once they sense this acceptance from others, there is no further need to defend themselves and then may turn their attention to others. Whatever the reason for this phenomenon occuring, there is no doubt that the concrete expression of Christian love could and should be the goal of any retreat experience.

The traditional retreat was properly focused on increasing the love of individuals for one another. In its best attempts, however, there was no opportunity during the retreat period itself to express genuine concern for others. The period was normally spent in attempts by the retreat master to reach this concept through exhortation. The first opportunity to demonstrate genuine Christian love was offered after the retreat was over and the stimulus was no longer present. If the exhortations were frustating or confusing in any way, the misunderstanding could not be discussed or shared. The retreat dynamic offers a totally new dimension in attaining the goals of all retreats by allowing an equal opportunity to simultaneously discover and practice new insights into communal life.

The qualities present in the Christian communities described in the Acts of the Apostles are not clearly known, but the descriptions that are offered suggest that much of the atmosphere generated was the result of the same kind of understanding and spontaneity which is the result of a successful group dynamic session. Certainly the externals which prompted men to remark that the Christians were known by their love for one another must have been the same kind of qualities discussed here. If the use of dynamics in retreats will create this same kind of love between retreatants, then to resist such a move would be to be blind to the most fundamental goal upon which the retreat is based.

A great deal is demanded of the individual leader attempting to unleash the dynamic inherent in every group. Far more than in the traditional retreat, the total personality of the retreat master will be crucial in the success or failure of such an attempt. He must demonstrate to everyone in the group the character-istics each individual is expected to attempt to achieve. The fact is that whether he desires such an end or not, the retreat master will establish the norm toward which group members will tend. Scientific studies have determined that the individuals in a group become more like the group leader as a result of their experience. This would be threatening enough in the normal group setting. In the retreat, he must not only be an example of the human virtues, but set the norm of Christianity for the group by his words and actions.

Unless the retreat master has firm convictions of his own and is committed to living the life of Christ at all times, it would probably be better for him not to attempt such a retreat. If he believes in his own personal growth as a Christian, however, he will find no more stimulating manner of increasing that same growth than through group interaction. Such a means may appear dangerous and demand significant risks at times, but the rewards are proportionately worthwhile.

The retreat master's Christian attitude demonstrated in both word and action is basic to the success of a retreat based on group dynamics, but his philosophical orientation will also help determine the extent to which the goals of the retreat are reached. If the retreat master genuinely does look toward all people as having worth and significance, he will have far less trouble creating within the retreatants a sense of trust in himself. He must, however, act as if he trusts others, not just verbalize this trust. When there is a subtle conflict between his stated trust in others and attempts to guide them himself, the retreat master is clearly manifesting an attitude which devaluates the person.

It might be pointed out that the philosophical orientation of the retreat master using group dynamics is not a static one in any sense. From whatever source and in whatever context he gains this respect for individual persons, the important consideration is that in a developmental manner his philosophical orientation tends to move in the direction of greater and greater respect for the individual. The nonreflective person might never question his respect for others, but those working hard for such an attitude know that such respect grows within the individual only at the cost of much pain and effort. The genuinely reflective person also knows this positive attitude toward others, and his ability is closely related to his growth and personal integration.

The best summary of the growth necessary for the successful retreat master would be to suggest that he must be in the process of becoming another Christ. Through close union with the scriptures, reflective meditation on Christ's personality, constant attempts to live with the mentality discovered in the scripture, the retreat master should, insofar as possible, reflect concretely to the retreatants the kind of mentality which was Christ's.

This chapter was written in an attempt to answer the charge that the introduction of group dynamics into the retreat is an attempt to weaken the religious orientation of the experience. Far from weakening the religious experience, the goal of retreat dynamics is to intensify the experience in a way which will offer greater challenges to both retreat master and retreatants. While the mode of expression has definitely changed, there need be no question concerning any lack of religious orientation in a retreat centered around the use of group dynamics.

REFERENCES

1. Lynch, William F. Toward a Theology of the Secular. *Thought,* 1966, XLI, 162, p. 349.
2. Ibid., p. 350.
3. Ibid., pp. 351-2.
4. Ibid., p. 354.
5. Ibid., p. 354.
6. Ibid., p. 356.

6. maintaining retreat values

One characteristic of a time of change is a certain undefined fear that permeates the atmosphere. This feeling is more easily perceived in some persons than others, but few completely escape the anxiety concerning the future when structures are changed. The person advocating a change in structure might seem unconcerned about difficulties involved, but in his more reflective moments he will admit that irrational emotions give him frequent misgivings concerning what he logically considers an important and necessary move.

It might seem reasonable to dismiss such feelings as irrational and of no consequence, but the emotions do have a basis in reality and need to be considered in order for us to understand our actions. One ought not to dismiss an emotion as though it did not exist simply because it does not fit into the intellectual pattern we have constructed for ourselves. On the contrary, unless we can recognize the existence and effects of our emotions, we are not in a position to evaluate properly what it is we are attempting to achieve by our actions. If we suppress an emotion connected with an action before giving it proper consideration, we are very likely to be overlooking an important aspect of that action which will have ramifications not only for ourselves, but also for the success or failure of the goals intended by the action performed.

The emotion of fear is a normal reaction to change, it would therefore be well worth considering seriously the underlying causes of such fear. The most obvious cause could be the lack of experience with a new situation which would be necessary to completely judge the success or failure implicit in the proposed change. Anyone who suggested that a proposed change of structures was certain to be more successful than established methods would reveal a distinct lack of understanding of the matter. The person proposing change might have a deep personal conviction that the move suggested must be attempted and will be successful; he must admit, however, that the new is an unknown and contains many unpredictable elements that might not have been properly weighed.

Fear is a part of man's natural reaction to the unknown. When familiar structures are removed, a real sense of insecurity develops until the new becomes more familiar. Even removing something unwanted leaves a certain amount of insecurity in its wake.

Another important though not so obvious reason for fearing change is reflected in the individual proposing the change. He has a vested interest in the success or failure of what he proposes. He is not likely to escape the feeling that he fails if the proposal fails. In order to bring a proposal to the point where it is considered by others, a person must make the proposal a projection of his own personality. One must always face some criticism for suggesting new approaches.

We cannot consider all possible reasons why anxiety accompanies change, but fear of the unknown and judgment by others are the most obvious. If apprehension concerning that which is new and untested goes beyond reasonable dimensions, it would be reasonable to suggest that the fear is a personal fear which has little to do with the statement of change itself. Many will identify their fear with something like a proposed structural change which is a far more acceptable rationale than their own personal fear. Assuming from this point on that objections are formed on a logical basis, we will consider the positive and negative reasons for a change in the retreat structure which has been a part of the Church for many years. It is sincerely hoped that each point will be weighed with an eye toward balancing the value of the new as opposed to the old rather than allowing an irrational fear which is based on insecurity to determine basic attitudes.

Let us look at the kind of fear which is part of the reaction many experience when considering a change in the basic retreat structure. The usual reason for opposing this change is the fear that some of the traditional goals may be lost in change. This is genuine reason to consider the change at some depth before moving in that direction.

There is no doubt that traditional means toward the sanctified goals of the retreat would be replaced by the method suggested; the goals, however, remain constant. One can easily see that there is a radical difference between the traditional retreat and one which employs the dynamic, but one must be sensitive in order to see just where that difference lies. This distinction between means and ends is difficult to discern at times, and it is not surprising that great difference of opinion will exist even after the issue has been thoroughly discussed.

Beyond the claim that the goals of the retreat are not changed by altering the means to those goals, there is a further claim here that the means used in the dynamic retreat are superior to those traditionally exercised. If such a claim proves to be true, there is reason to believe that the goals will be more surely attained by a greater number of retreatants. The matter of demonstrating whether or not these means are superior remains before us, but the effort to make such a decision would seem necessary in order to discover a more effective manner of drawing persons toward a true Christian experience.

All that can be accomplished in this discussion is a consideration of some goals which are central to a genuine retreat experience from a traditional point of view. Obviously it is impossible to consider all the goals which are intended to result from a genuine retreat. Anyone who has participated in a retreat knows well that the really effective retreat has so many ramifications that one would be hard pressed even to begin to list all of them. Furthermore, the fact that the positive results differ for each individual makes the task of understanding the goal of the retreat in its entirety all but impossible. With such realistic limitations placed upon our task, we will attempt to discuss a few of the goals a retreat offers to its participants with an eye to showing that modern retreat methods will offer retreatants an opportunity to attain these goals in more depth than ever previously possible.

One of the most obvious differences between a retreat based on group dynamics and the traditional form is the lack of silence in the former. Naturally the advisability of destroying the silence which has always appeared to be an essential part of a retreat will be questioned. We must therefore investigate the reason for the silence to discover whether any essential element has been eliminated.

The basic intent of imposed silence permeating the retreat atmosphere seems to lie in the reflectivity which will occur when one is alone with his own thoughts. The calm and silence of the retreat enables the participants to genuinely consider themselves in the deepest reaches of their thoughts and emotions. Because such an atmosphere also contained the religious connotation, such thoughts and reflections normally centered on their personal relationship with God and its multiple ramifications.

If we focus on reflectivity as the goal and silence as the means to attain it, then we are in a position to better understand the difference between a traditional and modern retreat. Creating an atmosphere in which one will be able to reflectively consider himself both as an individual and in relationship to God is equally the goal of both silence and group dynamics. In its very definition, group dynamics essentially attempts to create an atmosphere of reflectivity which allows one to better understand himself and the basic, underlying reason for his existence.

One of the goals of a group-centered leader is to look beyond the words a person uses to the intention which that same person has in using them. He must sense the distinction between an individual's verbal expression and the emotional impact with which he projects his words and phrases. Experience has proven that introducing such a dichotomy to persons normally produces a reflectivity at the deepest level. As a person begins to eliminate the distinction between what he intellectually and emotionally expresses, he normally begins also to discover himself in his true identity. Only through honest reflection upon himself can anyone begin to unite his emotional and intellectual life. The sensitivity of the leader in the group discussion will encourage individuals to search within themselves for an understanding of their words, actions, and emotions. This would appear to be an adequate definition of reflectivity.

After a brief orientation period, the leader's perceptiveness becomes infectious and other members of the group begin to become sensitive to more fundamental meanings which the content of the words suggests. It is difficult to remain unreflective in an atmosphere where this sensitivity prevails, and, more important, this reflectivity is more likely to produce positive results with so many persons anxious to help each individual discover himself at an emotional as well as psychological level.

Group dynamics promises a greater possibility of fruitful reflection than the imposition of silence. For example, a person might readily believe, in all honesty, that his prayer life offers him a great deal of fulfillment. If, for one reason or another, this were not true and he were consciously or unconsciously placing obstacles in the way of genuine communion with God, this will become obvious to the sensitive members in his attempt to express it. More than just pointing out such a discrepancy to the individual, the group could offer him reasons why they themselves find a fulfilling prayer life difficult. Many are helped to begin to better understand themselves and their relationship to God through such a process.

It would be well to mention that even in a retreat which is completely dominated by group discussion there must be some time available to all for personal reflection. If an individual were to spend lengths of time with others in discussion without having time available to sort things out personally, it would be reasonable to suspect he would retain a degree of confusion which could be more or less destructive to the reflective process. The major difference with the retreat based on the dynamic is that more than one means of inducing reflectivity is available.

Another fear which occurs to the individual who encounters

the group dynamic retreat for the first time is the reasonable fear that no one is really responsible to see to it that a certain amount of material is covered. If the pattern of leadership suggested for the retreat master does not readily lend itself to introducing certain basic ideas into the retreat, some get concerned that the retreat may lose something necessary for a genuine retreat experience.

In order to place this question in proper perspective, it is necessary to examine the present situation in the traditional retreat format. A retreat master with any kind of serious purpose in preparing for his retreats will outline carefully the amount of material he will attempt to cover during the time allotted. He will pick and choose the material he hopes to cover and the manner in which he expects to present that same material.

It is obvious from even a minimum amount of consideration of this method that all important aspects of man's relationship to God cannot be covered in a weekend, week, month, or even a lifetime. By considering nothing more than the radical difference in the material two different retreat masters choose to present, it is also obvious that there is little unanimity concerning what material is essential for a successful retreat. The different style of presentation which individuals will employ to convey identical points will further illustrate the contrast.

An analogy which will point up the dangers of the approach is the syllabus which has become such a dominant tool in education. In order to assure those in authority that all students will be exposed to the important material, a syllabus is used to give the instructor a certain number of classes in which to cover a given number of topics. The syllabus would be a valuable and effective tool for educators if persons learned according to some kind of timetable. But the fact is that human beings do not learn on schedule.

In another important way the retreat master is attempting to do the impossible without being fully conscious of the fact. As he ponders what material should be presented to this particular group and, more significantly, how it should be presented, he is attempting to predict the reactions of a large group of people. The motive for such reflection is commendable, but there is a note of manipulation in the process. It can readily be noted that such attempts lend themselves to insincerity. A person choosing topics and words to best convey the acceptance of predetermined conclusions is in danger of not being completely convinced of the same conclusion in its totality.

Even if we accept the ability of the retreat master not to stray from conclusions and the expression of conclusions which genuinely spring from honest personal reflection, one still runs the danger of addressing himself to topics which are not the most pressing in the life of those he is addressing. There is normally some consideration for the type of group addressed — nurses, lawyers, or religious — but there can be little insight into the person coming to the retreat as an individual. Since the meaning of the retreat implies touching individuals in that personal relationship they have with God, the retreat master who miscalculates concerning those things important for the personal growth of the group will necessarily make the retreat experience only minimally profitable for a large number of his retreatants.

By way of contrast, then, one can see the more obvious advantages of making group discussion an integral part of the retreat format. The assurance given by the attitude the retreat master brings to the group discussion that the questions and doubts of the group are the most important topics to be discussed, will help the group to gradually make known the difficulties they personally experience in attempting to develop a close union with God. By beginning with problems which personally preoccupy the group, there can be little doubt that they will feel more involved in the discussion and consequently the retreat experience.

In contrast to the manner in which the retreat master tells the group of retreatants the things they should do to draw closer to union with God in the traditional retreat, group dynamics offers him a chance to work with his retreatants to discover their solution in the context of their own formulation of the problem. If an individual retreat master is successful in allowing the group of retreatants to take the lead in determining what topics will be considered, there is less chance the retreatants will consider the experience irrelevant.

When the retreatant raises the topics for discussion, the retreat master himself has a better opportunity to become personally involved and encounter the retreat itself in a more personal manner. He can work with the retreatants in the same personal manner he approaches an individual. By working with one individual at a time in a group setting, the retreat master presents himself to the group in a much more human context than he would if he followed the classical method of lecturing before the group.

The more specifically spiritual aspects of the retreat can now be considered. The same obstacle to considering all goals continues to exist, but the aim will be to demonstrate that the goal remains intact in this dynamic form of retreat. The aim in introducing new means is not an attempt to discredit traditional forms, but rather to create as many paths as possible to reach the same goal.

We begin with an examination of prayer to have the maximum opportunity to discover the truth of these statements. The examination of prayer is in no way a criticism of traditional methods of prayer. All retreats emphasize by means of discussion and time allotted to it the need and value of a retreat to personally communicate with God. Another method of prayer is suggested for use during the retreat period only to increase the value and impact of such prayer.

In hearing many persons discuss the difficulty they personally experience trying to find meaning in their prayer life, it might be readily understood that difficulties in this area are as personal as the person encountering them. Beneath the expressions which suggest emptiness, meaninglessness, or lack of concentration, there normally lies a deeper cause which reflects the individual human condition from which any union with God must begin. Prayer requires such human qualities as concentration in order to make such prayer meaningful, it is not surprising, therefore, to discover that many of the problems also spring from difficulties the individual experiences in his everyday life.

One can thus readily see why a talk given on prayer and the blocks to prayer can be so inadequate for many. If the individual cannot express his own personal difficulties and hear of the difficulties others might be experiencing, he could readily find his own situation too terribly unique to find consolation in the necessary generalities of a talk given to a large group. We can also see the almost impossible task which lies before the retreat master. He may know that despite the uniqueness of each person's difficulty with prayer, but the most forceful presentation of the commonality of the problem is not very likely going to break through the emotional conviction of the individual. As with so many other aspects of life, the individual normally finds it difficult to believe that others face the same difficulty.

All have faced difficulties with prayer during their lives, so it is not unrealistic to draw on that experience in developing the dimensions of the problem. It does little good to offer more time for prayer to one caught in the arid period. More often than not, such extra time only compounds the problem by creating more opportunity for conflict. In order to break the vicious circle within which even the most devoutly religious person can find himself at times, it is necessary to get outside the normal framework for perspective on himself and his problem.

Many retreat masters find that there is no more effective way of relieving the depression many suffer regarding aridity in prayer than spontaneous prayer. Either because they are touched by the sincerity of another's open expression to God and before others or because they concretely hear another's difficulty in honestly expressing himself, many are able to place their own difficulties in proper perspective. A person who has gained the courage to speak to God while others listen has not only aided himself in honest expression, but has also shown others in a real way what communication with God can mean.

There is always a great degree of fear surrounding an open attempt to speak to God, spontaneous prayer must therefore be introduced into the retreat format with a great deal of caution. If there is the slightest degree of pressure exerted on anyone to participate, the effort will be strained and result in a negative reaction on the part of all. The retreat master must avoid any such pressure by drawing others to spontaneous expression through his own example. There will be little lasting resistance to his example if the atmosphere of the retreat is considered safe by those participating.

Prayer expression that is open to the reactions of others can become a powerful force which will create honest attempts at communion with God. Sincere and spontaneous prayer will be recognized immediately by the members of the group. Nothing can be more beneficial to many struggling in their inability to communicate with God than hearing the sincere expression of another.

The power of the Christian community to speak with God will remain overlooked unless the spontaneous prayers which are the most meaningful attempts to lift heart and mind to God are shared between persons. When one realizes concretely the strengths and weaknesses of others in their efforts to communicate, he can be heartened in his own human attempts which seem so inadequate at times. In the same manner which Christians aid one another in every other endeavor, they may also be valuable aids in bringing each other to God through this most powerful means of salvation.

Spontaneous prayer will always remain a secondary method of expression because of its peculiar nature, but that does not mean its value should be overlooked. Its expression demands the presence of a group, so it is all the more important that the retreat format include opportunity for such expression. The average Christian will not find the occasion for such expression outside of the retreat experience. If individuals were not allowed the exposure to this valuable opportunity during one of the few times they are in a position to use it, the retreat might readily lack a dimension which could be of utmost value in moving the retreatants ever closer to intimate union with God.

A great deal of personal time and effort has been put into

attempting to discover the proper means to begin group discussions. Articles from current journals were offered to some groups, others were stimulated by the thought-provoking questions and others were left to a variety of means to help precipitate discussion, but it gradually became evident that nothing was quite as powerful in opening a group as the requirement that they read a passage from St. John's gospel before gathering for discussion.

There were usually objections that meaningful discussion could come in many more creative ways. The resistance to gospel discussion was caused by the feeling that the stories were familiar and could offer no new insights to the retreatants. After a certain period of probing scripture in a personal manner, the only frustration experienced was the inability of the group to get beyond discussion of the first few verses offered for consideration.

Since the foundation of the Christian religion arises directly from scripture, man can undoubtedly reflect on its meaning indefinitely. More than the general knowledge scripture gives man in his endeavor to lead a fulfilling life, the Word is also intended as an individual statement for each man regardless of the age or condition in which he discovers himself. There can be little wonder at the meaning a group can uncover in an earnest search through the gospel story to find answers to personal conflicts concerning one's religious commitment. The experience of watching groups become involved in the personal meaning of a phrase or passage in scripture makes it easy to see the meaning scripture may have for individuals if they only approach it with the honesty and sensitivity which can be released in the dynamics of a retreat setting.

As experience with gospel discussion increases, it is easy to see the meaning scripture holds for the individual. Within the definite framework of scriptural meaning provided by the Church and her scholars, much personal meaning may be obtained which is an ever vital source for Christian life. If any one thing becomes obvious after a reflective consideration of the gospels, it is the absence of the feeling that the gospel cannot speak to modern man in his apparently unique situation.

However, many are not used to reflective reading of scripture, and the discussion technique becomes all the more valuable in developing an appreciation of its personal meaning. Each person may only, at best, be able to precipitate one personal reflection on a particular passage, but his will be one of many in the group. Joined to many such spontaneous reflections and penetrating their meaning, a sense of the impact scripture holds for man begins to grow.

There is a great need to create opportunities for scriptural discussion for the benefit of the many individuals who assume scripture to have a rather static message for man. Only in the context of a group gradually penetrating the meaning of a particular passage will many grow to realize the depth of wisdom contained within the scripture. When the impact of a particular passage begins to unfold before the group, it becomes more and more apparent that the message is dynamic and will never be completely penetrated in all its implications.

The retreat attempt to understand scripture demonstrates the same desire to reach traditional goals by modern means. Whatever the method used to accomplish the feat, the goal of giving persons an understanding and appreciation of scripture remains the same. There is no doubt that every retreat master has as his goal to transfer a love and appreciation of scripture to those with whom he works. The need to reflect is caused by his desire to use the best means available.

A retreat master who attempts to transfer personal appreciation of scripture to others by preaching to them of the fruits he has gathered from honest reflection may indeed inspire them and still fail to make such reflections aid in their growth towards a better understanding of the Word of God. Having the personal opportunity to reflect on the gospel is needed to avoid feeling threatened by such a task because of real or imaginary inadequacies. Sharing personal impressions in the presence of others and being able to seek help in understanding the meaning of such impressions builds confidence and desire which encourage one to delve deeper into scripture to find assistance in living out one's Christian commitment.

Experience has created the personal conviction that discussion of scripture is a powerful means to be used in retreats not only to understand scripture but also to realize personal potential. In order for it to attain its proper goal, however, the retreat master must be convinced of its value and convinced of its effectiveness. Since there is no absolute in the attempt to discover the best format for retreats, the "best" format for any retreat master is the one in which he is most comfortable. The only hope is that more will try to unleash group dynamics within the retreat so that they will be in a position to make an honest judgment.

The dominating purpose for writing this chapter was to assure those who are skeptical that there was no desire among the advocates of group dynamics to destroy the traditional goals of the retreat experience. A superficial glance at the new format might give some cause for concern along this line, but a more serious reflection upon the goals of a retreat should assure those who are dubious about modern retreat methods that a sharp break from tradition is just not in this case a reality. Only those who will not take the time and effort to reflect seriously about such novel approaches that retreat dynamics suggest will retain any lasting concern over creating new methods for the retreat.

Since the means suggested for the modern retreat are a break with recent tradition, it is not surprising that many would question whether or not they are introduced for the sake of novelty alone. Such novelty undoubtedly attracts many to a new format in retreats, but new approaches have the potential to extend beyond such an ephemeral state into a permanent role in the experience. This belief is dependant upon the strong conviction that the modern means do not in any way change the permanent goals of the retreat experience.

There is no attempt to hide from the fact that the modern retreat introduces means which are by comparison completely different paths leading to the traditional goals. There is, however, a firm conviction that such means are intended as alternate paths without any attempt to suggest that the more traditional means should be discarded or discontinued. The suggestion that group discussion should be introduced into a retreat format does not imply that the modern retreat has no place for the talks which have always been a dominant part of the retreat experience. Advocating certain times and places for discussion does not imply that periods should not be set aside for silent reflection. In short, a strong personal conviction would suggest that modern means should be introduced into the retreat in order to make it more effective in achieving the goal.

It would be impossible to determine to what extent such means should be introduced into all formats. The attempt to find an ideal framework would fail due to the individual temperaments and personalities of the retreat masters working through such a framework. Much of the problem with the traditional retreat format is its rigidity. Though some flexibility in the length and number of talks is allowed to the retreat master, the schedule of the day is largely determined for him. To do no more than structure a new rigid schedule for retreats would automatically forfeit much of the potential value in such a change.

We might emphasize this point by considering the retreat master who has neither the personality nor the temperament to be comfortable using modern methods in the retreat. If such a person were to use such methods regardless of personal inclination and ability, he would undoubtedly limit his own effectiveness as well as limit the effectiveness such methods might have for the retreatants in the future. The genuineness of the experience must come first in determining the format to be used or something important will be lost for all participants.

A distinction should also be made between the retreat master who, because of personal style, cannot use modern means effectively and the retreat master who simply will not. If a retreat master determines before any honest experience with such means that he will not attempt to use them, he is conceivably eliminating the possibility of giving himself and his retreatants a richer experience. But no amount of writing about such an experience will alone convince anyone of its worth; retreat masters must experience for themselves the value of the modern methods being proposed.

The fact is that many retreatants and retreat masters are finding the use of modern means a valuable method in enriching the retreat experience. Whether such means become standard practice in all retreats is not really the important issue. The important issue is whether all are willing to take an honest and reflective look at the retreat experience with an eye toward maximizing its effectiveness. Whether this reflection creates greater use of the means suggested here or eliminates their use altogether, the retreat will be richer because of such reflection. Nothing more can really be asked.

7.   retreat format

In order to establish a concrete setting in which to judge the retreat based on the dynamic, it is important to begin a more pragmatic consideration of the actual setting. General considerations give an insight into the goals in mind, but it is only through the more immediate questions of time and place that one really comes to grips with what is being suggested. Frequently the general agreement men reach is destroyed when the matter is actualized in the practical order.

In order to not establish a rigid framework within which all must operate, no exact schedule of the day will be suggested. Rather, a spectrum of possible approaches will be introduced so that the desire to establish the concrete will be tempered realistically by the need to adapt to the temperament and ability of the individual retreat master. With more than one way of introducing the dynamic into the retreat, a possible balance can be attained.

The important question to be answered here will be the extent to which the group discussion should be dominant in the retreat format. A consideration of this topic in depth should provide a foundation for answering all other questions. With an attempt to compare by contrast the many possible formats within the general consideration presented here, there should be a more realistic understanding of the ramifications the dynamic can have on the retreat experience.

The question that would immediately occur to a retreat master attempting to introduce group dynamics into his own personal format is how much of the retreat should be given over to group discussion. It is a question for which no hard and fast rule can be presented. Rather than even suggest a maximum or minimum, the discussion will rather focus upon factors which would limit the amount of time given over to such discussion.

The dominant factor in determining such an answer will be the temperament and ability of the retreat master. If the retreat master is dissatisfied, unhappy or even uncomfortable with the format suggested, such a format cannot be considered right for the situation. We must recognize the critical importance of the relaxed attitude and conviction a retreat master must bring to the experience in order to be effective.

It should be admitted immediately that this discussion will stress the value of using every available minute of the retreat for group discussion. Outside of the necessary time given over to sleeping, eating, the sacraments, prayer and personal reflection, the most valuable use of time during retreat is spent in group discussion. This would normally mean that something like eight hours a day would be spent with groups in direct attempts to unleash the dynamic with the assembled community.

The idea of dominating the retreat with group discussion has, in my personal experience, developed gradually. As comfort with unproductive periods and apparently disruptive elements in the discussion grew, more and more time was given over to such discussion. An increased number of statements attesting to the value of the experience from the retreatants reinforced this progression. As time spent in group discussion increased, the conclusions of the discussions tended to produce more creative insights into personal spirituality. With greater time set aside for group discussion the experience proved more rewarding for all who participated.

It might be well to emphasize the fact that without experience few would or could be capable of entering upon such a plan. It is anticipated, however, that as experience with any degree of discussion grows, there will be a tendency to increase the amount of time given over to such discussion. Total discussion should be considered the culmination point of positive experience with group dynamics, not the starting point. With such a goal in mind as the ideal toward which he might tend, it will be suggested that many retreat masters will gradually grow in the method to the point that no other format will be satisfying.

Since groups of forty or more are difficult to manage in nothing but large group atmosphere, even the most ardent disciple of the large group setting will break such a group into smaller units for some of the retreat time. Such a breakdown might occur by breaking the larger group into small units of about six for some period of the retreat. Another approach would be to divide the group in half and work with one group in a large group setting while the other is in the small discussion unit. While many creative approaches immediately occur, it should be remembered that to the extent one breaks the total group into smaller units he is weakening the possibility of total community cohesion.

There are, as has been said, many limiting factors to attaining the goal of large group setting during the entire retreat such as the ability and temperament of the retreat master, the openness of the group, and the size of the group on the retreat. Since cohesion and a sense of community most surely grows between those members who work together, the ideal of this sense growing within the total community assembled may not always be best attained due to such limitations. With the ideal clearly in mind, however, the best compromise within the limiting factors present will be immediately evident.

It should be noted that there is an easy tendency to suggest limitations where they do not in fact occur. A group of one hundred might immediately appear to be completely unresponsive to direct encounter, but groups of this size have been successfully instilled with all the positive aspects of the dynamic described earlier. Encounter with such a large group is not suggested as normal in the retreat context; it should be noted, however, that limitations on the application of the dynamic are not fixed. Depending upon the personal freedom of the retreat master, no limitation really exists in his ability to create a sense of community.

The attempt to emphasize the importance of the large group context for retreats might make it appear that there is a corresponding desire to negate the impact small groups may have on retreatants. Nothing could be farther from the truth. It is an established fact that in small groups there is a greater possibility of opening the individual to himself and others. The individual feels a greater sense of security and freedom in the context of the intimate relationship naturally formed in a small group atmosphere than he would in larger groups. With this greater sense of freedom, there is no doubt that the goals of the dynamic will be more surely discovered in less time than would be possible in the larger group.

If the entire retreat were in the context of the subgroups, however, many disadvantages would normally result. The most obvious implication of no large group atmosphere is the lack of contact between members of the retreat. In his own unique way, each member of the community gathered is experiencing growth or obstacles to growth which he might share with others. Sharing unique experiences with others makes them become valuable aids in releasing genuine feelings which are the occasion of insights necessary for growth individually and collectively. If such insights were only shared with a few, the remaining retreatants would lose something invaluable in their retreat experience.

If the force of circumstances limits the retreat master to a way that makes it necessary for the total group to break down into smaller units for part of the retreat period, it follows that not all of these groups will have the benefit of an experienced leader. Even leaderless groups will select their own leader and a dynamic will grow within the group eventually, but the process will be slower and develop less effectively than it would if a skilled and experienced leader were present. The experienced leader, by his perceptiveness and sensitivity, would be able to help the group discover the means necessary to precipitate dynamics within the group. Through trial and error attempts to move toward more meaningful discussion, a group will attain the same goal with less speed and total impact. The fact of the matter is that many occasions will not allow the large group setting to dominate the total retreat. When such a necessity appears to present itself, it should be kept in mind that the total experience will be correspondingly weakened.

Until this point in the discussion the needs of the group have been emphasized as the crucial element determining the amount of large and small group discussion which should be allowed during the course of a retreat. This viewpoint emphasizes the ideal setting for the retreat. Viewing the same circumstances with other areas of emphasis in mind will highlight the realistic limitations that are placed on the ideal. Probably the most important limitations to be considered sympathetically are the personal limitations of the retreat master.

A brief review of the role of the retreat master in leading a group-centered discussion will show the serious demands such leadership lays on the person. In order to focus the attention of the group in on itself, the retreat master must shift the emphasis of responsibility back to the group. While really understanding that they are now responsible for all progress made within the group is difficult for the members to accept, it is a much more difficult transition for the leader. Especially when the discussion begins to lag or progress is slow, the retreat master will experience the strong feelings that the only solution for moving beyond such periods will be accomplished by his own decision to step in and press the group beyond their temporary block. As long as he is able to keep such feelings in perspective, positive growth within the group will not be disturbed.

The retreat master has several ways of breaking the tension such emotions may reach at times. The inexperienced retreat master who attempted to lead two four-hour discussions a day on any given day would have to be temperamentally exceptional to avoid being overwhelmed by his innate desire to dominate the group at times. When one accepts the fact that there is a limit to the amount of time he can sustain a group-centered outlook, he realizes that his only recourse is to break the periods of discussion into smaller units.

One of the more realistic ways to limit the amount of time

given over to such discussion is to take advantage of the breaks in the schedule which superficially appear necessary to all participants. By breaking the large group into smaller discussion units or introducing the coffee break into the large group setting, the leader will find it easier to sustain a proper perspective on the movement of the group. Many other means of maintaining balance will naturally occur which should be used insofar as they are necessary.

No one would blame a retreat master for using the real and artificial breaks in the schedule in order to relieve some of the pressure that results from long periods of group-centered leadership, but he should understand that in doing so he is reducing the possible effectiveness of such discussions. By introducing such breaks into the discussion, the retreat master may save himself from becoming a disruptive force in the dynamic which is growing within the group. As his experience with such groups increases, however, he must constantly challenge his own capacity so that breaks will be a matter controlled by him rather than something he is forced to do.

The present analysis might suggest that the longest discussion without a break is necessarily the best, but this is certainly not the case. Looking at the matter of discussion length from the vantage point of one inexperienced in such group work, it can justifiably be suggested that many rationalizations come to the surface naturally for limiting such discussion. It is not uncommon to discover on reflection, however, that such rationalizations spring from the individual's inability to rid himself of the feeling he is completely responsible for the group. To the extent that he manifests such an attitude to the group, the members simply will not begin to grow in that sense of cohesiveness and interdependence upon which group dynamics is built.

In attemping to discover what makes long discussion periods difficult for all who participate in them, one could point to many factors which are possible causes. A few will be highlighted here as possible explanations of the difficulty, but there is no attempt to suggest that such explanations are unique or even the most crucial in determining any given period difficult for the individual or group. The suggestions here rather refer to reflections on personal experience which seem plausible and consistent with previous discussion.

While many groups have some difficulty beginning discussion, the earliest phase of discussion is usually marked by an easy and enthusiastic tendency to move discussion forward rapidly. In the earliest phase persons generally express an earnest ambition to discuss not only ideas but their personal reflections on such ideas. After a certain period of such openness and enthusiasm, there normally follows a period of time during which progress apparently ceases.

Such dry periods are often passed by a lack of any meaningful expression, but other forms of stagnation sometimes present themselves. One of the most difficult expressions of such stagnation is an argument between the members. Often the argument is expressed over an objectively inconsequential point, but not uncommonly it represents a hostility between certain members of the group. The leader's impulse to take the responsibility to rectify the situation is most intense at such a period, but even success in ending the argument externally will normally only postpone the need to express these same feelings at a later time.

In a more subtle way, group members may take leave of progress by use of less obvious means. One of the devices most frequently used to escape introspection is the tendency to intellectualize. Because the discussion has become too dangerous or is becoming too burdensome to the individual, he avoids expressing personal reactions and begins citing authorities.

The escape from further facing personal feelings in this manner is generally considered something undesirable because it hinders the immediate progress the group is capable of making, but such a pause is necessary from time to time in the normal progress of a group. In the very nature of the task being undertaken, it is understandable that pauses to reflect on the situation will arise. If a group is genuinely in the process of discovering its own identity both individually and collectively, it is moving into areas previously unexplored. It would be exceedingly insensitive of any leader not to anticipate periods where a great deal of caution must be exercised.

In any type of so-called unproductive period, the leader must be intensely aware of himself and sensitive to the doubt being generated within the group. While he must relax in the anxious moments such periods naturally generate, he must also periodically offer the group opportunities to pass over these periods by offering subtle suggestions which will make them aware of their lack of progress. When the usefulness of the pause is accomplished, the members will themselves recognize the meaninglessness of their discussion and move on provided that they are not pressed to move too rapidly by the leader. The more relaxed and experienced the leader, the easier it will be to make such transitions.

If we were to attempt to express any dominant reason for the discussion's coming to an impasse from time to time we would have to center our attention on the difficult nature of such honesty. There is little emphasis placed in our present social structure on the value of sharing with others our genuine feelings and reactions to the joys and frustrations we encounter in our daily lives. In sharp contrast to the value of sharing honestly with others, there is an undefined fear which dominates many when one even suggests such openness.

One explanation for feeling a sense of fear in the face of openness is that one often thinks he cannot trust others with a certain kind of truth about himself. Lacking trust in others, it is not surprising that individuals must hesitate at times before opening themselves further. Only by taking time to weigh the dangers and rewards involved in honestly confessing certain truths about himself and his relationship to God can any sensitive person move forward in such a sensitive area.

Underlying man's apparently innate fear of revealing his natural and supernatural nature to others is, more often than not, a more fundamental conviction that others could not possibly accept the person hidden beneath the facades and masks that dominate his daily life. By revealing honestly his weaknesses and the rather tenuous relationship he has with God, he feels that others must necessarily dismiss him as of no consequence and unworthy of their love. The fact is that only by revealing such human weaknesses will others be able to identify with him. As long as a series of facades generates a person without the emotions which are the common lot of men, no genuine bond of love will develop which may alone aid man to overcome his weak and all too human nature.

Another reason for developing long discussion periods is the recognition of a new milieu which develops within the group atmosphere. If the dynamic begins to grow within the group setting, there is a real difference between the time spent within the group and that passed outside of the discussions. In a successful attempt to unleash the dynamic present when any group gathers, it will become clear that group members are more honest with one another, will feel closer to one another, will be more sensitive to the needs of all, and, in general, allow the love which is part of a true Christian community to actualize itself.

As such dimensions are recognized within the group, it becomes increasingly obvious that it is important to sustain the group milieu as long as possible. There is a certain lack of reality surrounding the group atmosphere in which genuine feelings begin to develop, but the experience is invaluable in presenting the goal of a genuine Christian life to the participants. By breaking the sessions into small units of time, there is the danger that the sense of community will only be partially revealed. In a true Christian community, there is a necessity to live with frustration as well as reward, with joy and sorrow, with anxiety as well as serenity. By unnecessarily curtailing the amount of time spent in the midst of the experience, there is a real danger that an idealistic concept of what true community can and does mean will remain with the participants. Despite his tendency to limit the length of the experience, the retreat master should be well aware of the dangers implicit in following such inclinations too readily.

For reasons discussed previously there will be no attempt to outline a retreat schedule in detail. Not only would such a schedule limit the latitude of experience possible; but it would also introduce the kind of rigidity such innovations should carefully avoid. From the discussion of the amount of time a leader might best set aside in a retreat schedule for group work, it is hoped that the determining factors governing such a decision have become clear. By applying the other principles previously discussed most decisions necessary to plan details of such a program should present no serious obstacle. Though a few more specific considerations will be viewed in the light of the principles already suggested, there will be no attempt to cover every decision that might arise in a specific format.

In order for the Mass to gain its proper central focus in the context of the retreat, a necessary emphasis must be placed on the active participation of the retreatants in the celebration. Since we are living in an age in the Church which emphasizes participation, the retreat should have incorporated into the liturgy a maximum degree of participation. Because the retreat period offers the time and leisure which allow a greater degree of participation than is possible in the daily life of most individuals, it is the natural occasion to emphasize and experiment with forms of participation normally restricted by the circumstances.

Since the retreat format which emphasizes the dynamic naturally creates a greater sense of community among the participants than they normally experience, it is important that their sense of involvement in the Mass and liturgy keeps pace. If the retreatants become seriously involved in the dialogue with one another, a ritualistic presentation of the liturgy can become an obstacle rather than an aid in gaining spiritual insights which normally result from such an experience. The strength and power of the liturgy overly constricted by ritualistic demands could unnecessarily remain secondary in the aid which it could offer to one's advance in his relationship with the Christian community.

While a full participation at Mass is crucial to the retreat experience, it is just as crucial that the actual forms of participation be introduced as a result of group decision. Not only might the introduction of new forms of participation follow from group decision; but forms the individuals have already experienced could be reviewed. With an opportunity to allow the individuals who participate in the Mass to become more closely united in the ceremony, the retreat can offer a unique degree of participation. Not only is such intensity of participation desirable, but in this kind of experience it becomes vital in order to place the Mass in its proper context.

As a sense of community grows within the retreatants, the concept of community worship is understood with greater clarity. When he participates in offering the Mass while he is engaged in the process of developing his understanding of the emotional bonds which genuinely unite a member of a Christian community, he naturally grows in an understanding of what communal worship can and should mean.

Since the retreat format presented here suggests that the dominant experience in the retreat is the leaderless discussion, it may appear that the only means of direction available for the retreat master is the determination of the topics to be discussed. It is important to realize, however, that the importance of introducing topics can be easily overemphasized. After discussing a few aspects of this function in the retreat, it is hoped that proper perspective will be gained.

Viewing the possibility of such direction from a negative standpoint, it will be important to recall the basic function of a group-centered leader. In order for him to fulfill his basic role of diffusing leadership in the members of the group, it is vital that he not guide the discussion away from the direction toward which it tends. Group discussion can never be forced to develop along any predetermined line, and the tendency to overemphasize the importance of choosing discussion topics could supply the leader's ignorance of his proper role.

By suggesting a great concern for the exact topics which will be discussed, a leader indicates a further tendency to restrict discussion to this particular topic for a given period of time. Though such a tendency may not even be fully realized by the retreat master himself, there is strong indication that the success of the retreat experience will be weakened by even a subtle tendency to encourage a discussion to follow a certain predetermined pattern. It is the success or failure of the retreat master in such obscure aspects within the retreat that will determine the strength of the dynamic he is able to release.

Before developing this point further, it might be well to footnote the preceding statements with a clarification. Though the leader's tendency to want to adopt more familiar forms of leadership may weaken his effectiveness, he would be dishonest and ultimately less effective by forcing himself to adopt a stance which is totally uncomfortable. He would be dishonest, for example, to suggest that the determination of the topics for discussion were not important for personal reassurance if they are. The most one can hope for under the circumstances is the recognition by the individual that such tendencies do restrict his effectiveness. By gradually bringing such tendencies to the conscious level and properly evaluating them one is better able to adopt the techniques necessary in realizing the most effective retreat experience. The retreat master will certainly become singularly effective in his methods when he is able to easily display such honesty about personal feelings.

Since the danger implicit in overemphasizing the importance of which topics are discussed has been the major focus until now, it would be well to point out the genuine significance of carefully determining which topics should be discussed. Because discussion in the context of group dynamics is unstructured by its very nature, it is not surprising to find group members following any bit of structure offered by the leader. One could only find the point confusing if he had not experienced the desire to escape the sense of responsibility which the unstructured atmosphere thrusts upon the individual. At times during the discussions, this tendency is so strong that group members will follow even irrational suggestions rather than face the burden of deciding for themselves the future lines of development. One can readily see the danger of such a situation. Though this danger will be discussed in more depth in a future chapter, it will now be suggested that the leader would do well to consider to what degree he is willing to leave the experience unstructured.

A decision by the retreat master to follow a certain outline will be carefully followed by the retreatants in most cases. By giving some thought to what discussion might best follow on the humanity of Christ, for example, the retreat master could encourage the continuity of discussion rather than any abstract logical continuity which might force a break in previous thought patterns. There is no doubt that the retreat master is at a disadvantage in attempting to predict the outcome of any discussion in advance. There is good reason to suggest, therefore, that topic introduction itself may hinder the natural flow which has more immediate meaning to participants in the retreat experience.

If one were to consider the opposite extreme in the matter of topic introduction, he would be in a position to properly evaluate the potentially disruptive elements such introductions might pose. The opposite extreme of introducing topics naturally suggests that there is no need to introduce topics for discussion at all. While such a suggestion naturally disturbs many at first sight, the fact is that the normal and natural flow from one discussion to another without topical introduction.

With a little experience in leading open discussions, a retreat master gradually senses the flow that naturally occurs from one discussion to the next. If he becomes aware of the underlying questions that develop in one session, for example, he will find the group members returning to this implicit or explicit problem in the next discussion to continue the search for an effective solution. Such a flow is often subtle and a good deal of sensitivity and patience must be exercised in order to discover the main trend at times. As such sensitivity develops, however, the leader may offer a great deal of assistance to a group in attempting to move toward its own solutions.

In attempting to understand how one can allow a group to move in its own direction and still be sure that it will "cover the important ground," nothing will substitute for experience. Given the freedom to move in any direction it chooses, a group will come to grips with all important issues that would be covered in any retreat format. The difference is that when groups are allowed to exercise their own control over the movement, they will emphasize or deemphasize points according to the impact such topics genuinely have in their lives. Because they are solely responsible for the direction of discussion, they will further be personally involved in such discussion and its conclusions. One cannot prove logically that groups will act in this manner, and it must be left to individual experience to discover such truth. If anyone gives a group the opportunity to prove these points, however, there is little doubt that the results will be positive.

It might be pertinent to recall at this point in the discussion that personal preference has made St. John's gospel the point of departure for recent retreats. In line with the discussion on this point, there is nothing which is more stimulating for discussion than the contents of this gospel. While the passages easily stimulate much thought on the part of all, there is seldom much repetition of the ideas expressed. This gospel in particular tends to create food for thought which is relevant for each individual willing to take the time and effort to reflectively consider its implications.

With any approach that allows a group to explore the questions pertinent to its life situation, there are numerous opportunities for the views and experiences of the retreat master to be introduced. Since the group will normally spend most of its time in a process of search, innumerable questions will be asked of the retreat master. If he reacts by offering a reflective comment which bears the mark of honesty and resists tendencies to dogmatically close the issue with a direct answer, he will be able to preach to the group in a genuine sense without interrupting the flow of the discussion. A leader who demonstrates his honest attempt to work with the group toward an answer will be able to constantly test his own reactions to ultimate questions as well as offer immediate aid to the group involved in the quest for truth.

Though the discussion on this point does not present any concrete answers concerning the best way to stimulate discussion, it is sincerely hoped that a certain amount of insight will be offered to the individual in his attempts to adopt techniques which will best express his own personality and temperament. The true retreat dynamics is an attempt to allow the participants an opportunity to release their natural tendency to grow both naturally and supernaturally. It is hoped, therefore, that the retreat master will also be in a constant state of growth as a result of his participation in the experience. If such growth occurs as a result of his experience, it would be expected that specific formats would constantly change as a result of his unique development.

If there is any point developed within this chapter which is worthy of special emphasis, it is that the retreat format must conform itself to the personality of the retreat master. Everything discussed in this consideration is founded on the premise that the leader is of central importance in any proposed change of the retreat. Only when the change is a genuine attempt to allow the retreat master the possibility of growth will such change be desirable.

When the retreat master is concerned about the external setting of the retreat to the extent of losing contact with the retreat participants, the experience can have little or no chance of being an occasion of spiritual growth. Of primary importance in making the retreat a valuable period for all participants is the degree to which interpersonal relations may develop. The fact that there is genuine reason to suspect some leaders will press themselves into an unfamiliar format without the preparation necessary for properly understanding the rationale underlying such change. It is not surprising, therefore, to hear of many retreat masters being disillusioned with early attempts at new formats.

Since the basic reason for suggesting more discussion and

the like in a retreat is to increase the amount of interpersonal contact between all participants, one can readily understand that when the format creates restrictions on such contact all will be dissatisfied. If one were to accept the fact that all retreat formats depend for their success upon the degree of contact between the participants and the retreat master, such a conclusion would not be difficult to accept. It is certainly clear that the underlying explanation for introducing group dynamics into the retreat is to increase this basic contact during the retreat experience. If this move were to create the opposite effect and increase the lack of communication between participants, any degree of success would be unlikely.

Since the introduction of group dynamics is intended to intensify interpersonal relations between the retreat master and the participants, it may seem contradictory to suggest the possibility of this move destroying rather than creating such contact. As we realize such growth occurs normally when the atmosphere is considered safe for such exploration it is not surprising that even occasions created for such growth will have the opposite effect. Anyone who thinks that one creates an atmosphere for such growth by merely making structural changes is making a serious mistake. Not only must the atmosphere be warm and friendly, but the individuals who are to participate in that atmosphere must be at ease with themselves and one another.

If the retreat master is disturbed and unhappy about the structure to which he must adapt himself, such emotions are easily conveyed to the retreatants. While his discomfort could be sensed under any circumstance, it will be particularly evident in the context of the unstructured experience. His goal is to act as an example of the genuine Christlike interest and understanding the retreatants are to have for one another, and any preoccupation with externals will be particularly destructive to the goals of the dynamic. Since individuals cannot always control their emotions intentionally, it is crucial that the retreat leader be conscious of himself and not attempt to structure a retreat too far out of line with his taste and inclination.

If the retreat master were to go to the other extreme and not introduce any innovation into the pattern already established, he would be in danger of suggesting the opposite extreme to the participants. Any neglect in constantly challenging himself with fresh approaches will create a danger of transmitting a sense of apathy to the retreatants. If one were to produce static formulation for ingestion, he would have little chance of suggesting the kind of growth and excitement which Christianity must have if it is to have any permanent effect on the lives of those living according to its principles.

If there is any one thing which has led to the static and self-contained image the Church created for itself in the preconciliar age, it is the impression rampant among Catholics that they were guardians of a set of given truths which they must safeguard but not consider with honesty. In order to "think with the Church," a great deal of care must be exercised in even private consideration of such immutable verities. The unfortunate part of this fact was not so much that the "truths" themselves remained static in a changing world, but rather that religion had less and less influence on the lives of persons within the Church.

As the world became more and more involved with the great moral issues of our time particularly those involving the basic dignities of the human person, the Church remained in the background instead of forming the basis of moral leadership which Christ has left in our keeping. Without the sense that the Church is in the same process of growth that we see evolving on all sides, we become the pharisees of the age — keeping strict account of our legal framework in order to escape responsibility for the human suffering which surrounds us.

If there is any one thing which the retreat dynamics attempts to release within its participants, it is a new sense of vitality for religion and its impact on personal life. When the retreat experience awakens an understanding of the impact religion can and should have in the personal life of each individual, it will have begun the enormous task of making religion relevant again in the lives of Christians. If retreats continue to perpetuate the image of a Church aloof from the concerns of society, it would be better to discontinue the practice altogether. Only when the experience speaks to individuals as persons in unique human situations will the genuine relevancy of religion open before them. We can expect nothing but an increasingly irrelevant role for religion in our time without such attempts.

8. the retreat experience

At the end of the retreat period, experience has proven the value of requesting that each participant write a brief personal impression of the retreat and its implications. This kind of retreat is so unstructured that it is often difficult to gain an overall impression of its impact. By carefully reading through such statements, however, it is normally possible to get an impression of the impact of the experience.

A careful reading of such comments will normally give, more than just an overall impression of the retreat's impact, an insight into improvements that could be made. Though any overt criticism normally is in the form of suggesting minor structural changes, a careful consideration of the rationale for such suggestions often brings to light a temperamental difficulty with personal attitudes of the retreat master. A leader who will take such criticism seriously can gain insight into himself and grow in self-understanding. Such growth will not only aid his own natural and supernatural development, but it will make it possible to reach more retreatants with each new attempt.

On a more positive note, such statements can also give the retreat master some indication of his effectiveness in unleashing the dynamic within the retreat. If there is a common consensus of positive orientation toward others in the group in most of the statements, it would strongly suggest to the leader that he has been successful in developing the group consciousness which is one of his basic goals. The same holds true for just about any of the goals suggested as important to the experience desired.

Since the statements of their nature must remain brief, it

need not be surprising to find some elements which the leader feels need not be mentioned. For any number of reasons peculiar to the experience, the factor most important in making the retreat a success may not be noted by any of the participants. It is not surprising, therefore, that one might suggest that while such statements can be of great aid they need not necessarily be the ultimate criteria by which to judge the total effect.

In suggesting these short impressions may not be the best indication of the retreat's impact, we are also running the danger of permitting an individual to read them rapidly and without much reflectivity. Such an approach could conceivably permit a retreat master to overlook a valuable aid in discovering the degree to which he reached his intended goal. This is all the more dangerous because a first reading of most statements leaves much to be desired if one is looking for a complete insight into the dynamics of the process. Most of the statements will give the careful and reflective reader a hint as to what part of the experience was most valuable to each individual.

In selecting some statements for consideration in this chapter, we will not only have a chance to review the principles upon which a successful retreat is based, but also view those same qualities from the eyes of the participants. The hope is to allow the individual to view the experience in a manner similar to one who has actively participated in the actual format. Though nothing can actually substitute for the experience, it is hoped that the statements of participants will move us closer to its actual dimensions.

We might first of all consider a few statements which attempt to describe the basic atmosphere of the retreat and the reasons for its existence. In attempting to describe the features which underlie the growth of an "atmosphere of acceptance," we have made much of the attitude displayed by the leader. In the words of one Sister who gained much from the experience, there is a strong feeling that the leader had much to do with creating an atmosphere of acceptance.

I came to this retreat with modest hopes. I leave with the con-

viction that I can never again return to the silent passive
retreats of old. It has been a tremendous experience. I hope
to carry it with me. Your sincere acceptance of us made us
retaliate with acceptance for you, your methods and "ourselves." You made a bullseye!

Even if the "everyday" routine lay heavy on me again, they
can't quite lick me.

While the very brevity of the statement does not allow the
sort of analysis which has previously described the connection
between the acceptance of the leader and the atmosphere of the
group, it clearly links the two with a sense of conviction which
needs no such analysis. Within the context of the retreat, such
deep and sincere convictions are developed concerning many
aspects of the experience and of life generally. The retreat
atmosphere which permits such reflections will be filled with
statements of conviction which help all participants to begin
a new life of growth both naturally and supernaturally.

In discussing the retreat atmosphere to date, not much has
been said concerning its overall effect upon the participants. The
atmosphere will necessarily be experienced subjectively and to
express on description for all participants would be somewhat
presumptuous. Rather than leave the matter completely vague,
however, we quote from one Brother who found a relaxed tension in the atmosphere.

I think that the retreat has been a very interesting experience
but as far as any concrete results I have none. I feel that the
atmosphere was one of a very relaxed tension which created
the right formula for group discussion. In previous retreats
I felt almost restricted by the *forced* silence. I also feel that
group discussions — both small and large — were a real sign
of what men of God can do — be open, honest, and filled
with love.

In describing the "relaxed tension" he felt during the retreat,
this Brother is undoubtedly expressing the experience of many.
The active participant will feel a tension in the air even though
the emphasis has been on the calm and relaxation all must

experience if they are to open themselves to others. Before one can ever hope to begin honest exploration of inner thoughts and emotions, he must sense that the atmosphere is safe for such explorations. Depending upon the degree to which he is anticipating opening himself to the group, he must realize a corresponding sense of trust. Only when he genuinely feels that he can trust others, will he be able to express personal doubts and fears about himself and his relationship with God. Despite the degree to which he anticipates that others will respect his confidence the thought of such openness will always create a tension within. It is not at all surprising that the Brother quoted here would suggest that he simultaneously feels tense and relaxed. Though such a feeling is by no means universal, it would not be surprising to find many expressing the same apparently paradoxical description of the retreat atmosphere.

If the retreat master is minimally effective in creating the proper atmosphere within the format he finds suitable, there will be an opening up of one person to another. Many degrees of openness will be generated as the retreat progresses. The first sign of success in the experience will be the expressed realization by the participants that they have missed a good deal by their self-centered approach to others. In the words of one participant, such acceptance of others only begins when one is able to look honestly at himself first.

> The retreat had a positive value for me. It made me stand back and take a real look at myself, and to accept what I saw and place the real me before others. I feel the group was necessary for me to accomplish this. It is amazing to see how similar the ideas and problems of the different group members can be.

Such honesty with oneself creates a concurrent ability to accept others for what they are. In the normal approach to life, we are all too willing to judge others by the same standards we use for ourselves. By moving too swiftly to judge without attempting to understand the reasons for an individual's approach to life, we are clearly violating the basic admonition of Christ that we not judge others lest we also be judged.

One novice gained some insight into his attitude which kept others from becoming a part of his life. In his own words, he expresses the conviction that the retreat experience opened him up to "the reasons why people are what they are."

> This retreat was good for me because I learned a little more about myself. I learned a lot about how others think; I strengthened my belief to accept people for what they are at that time, not for what they were. On second thought, there are many reasons why people are what they are, especially the less fortunate. These must be considered. I think the biggest thing about this type of a retreat is that it gets into the open the attitudes people have for certain subjects. The atmosphere as a result is one of charitable and understanding acceptance.

If the retreat is to be a genuinely religious experience, it must transcend this level of personal acceptance. We will see that the impact for the retreatants does touch the realm of love for Christ in self and others as the discussion progresses. In looking at the new openness displayed toward others, we must not forget that such is the fundamental Christian message. In attempts to know and love others, one is fulfilling the basic command of Christ to love one's neighbor as oneself. The religious impact of such acceptance of self and others becomes a little more clear when it is articulated in terms of love of neighbor.

> I personally believe that this retreat has been good because now I have a better understanding of why I'm here and how I'm to reach God. Also, I believe I have more confidence in speaking with others, especially about pertinent things. I feel I've come to love my neighbors just a bit more, instead of having so much self-love.

Though it is being emphasized that the very first stage of growth within the context of the retreat is a new dimension of openness to others, one should not forget that even this beginning will come slowly and will involve a great deal of risk on the part of the retreatants. One who grows beyond the relationship he has maintained with others will do so in spite of fear and because of trust which was previously unrealized. In articulating the cost of growth, one student pinpoints well the risk involved.

> The point of the retreat is to grow or become. To do this, fear must be overcome. Perhaps the main cause of fear is a lack of real conviction. We must understand others to grow. Growth demands trust and sometimes our trust will be turned against us and this is when we will have to become a fool for Christ. We must still grow even in failure.

If one is genuinely sensitive to the struggle that many must encounter in order to make even minimal gains in opening to others at times, the results can be spectacular. From very slow beginnings, some have found the atmosphere safe enough to move rapidly toward the end of the retreat to a sense of openness which is the foundation of group consciousness. From what must have been a very slow start, one Sister found enough safety and trust among others to genuinely grow to a new realization of community awareness.

> Perhaps you would say that St. Peter's first day of preaching would get second billing when you witness the conversion during your retreat.

> I am not a talker except with a few and those only whom I trust but I found myself making speeches — the only thing lacking was the house top. I have lived in a community most of my life and never before really experienced what a community can mean to its members.

> Personally — well I don't think my inner fire will go out, never. I know I speak for several.

Though it is basically impossible to share anything personal with a group and not begin to build a sense of community, many are not clearly aware of how closely united these two concepts really are. Even the first experience of community is an individual experience and many are not able to distinguish between personal insight and a fresh experience of community concern. In his discussion of the personal value such sharing gave him, one student does not mention the dimension the group offered to his own personal experience.

> I believe that this has been one of the most interesting retreats I have ever been on. Mainly because of the experience that was made available to people that were looking for them.

> Most of the questions came from you, but the answers came from us. It made me realize that everyone has a lot to share with us and that group discussion is a very effective way of getting people to open up and share their experiences and insights.

The fact of not mentioning the new dimension which the group was able to offer to his insights does not mean the individual has lost the value of that dimension. It does suggest that some are not used to thinking in terms of the community consciousness. We speak a great deal of the need for a Christian community; however, one might suggest that many do not recognize even the most fundamental dimensions of its reality. In discussing the communal aspect of the retreat, one Brother focused on the use of such techniques to solve problems.

> The topics we discussed were very timely and (to use a cliché) relevant to our problems here at X. I am sold on group dynamics as a means, not an end, of arriving at a better community understanding of problems that we tend to think are unique but are really very common. I have learned how to listen a little better to others, to realize that others are talking from their own background and environment just as I hope they understand the same of me.

His new awareness of others and a growth in the ability to communicate with them gave this Brother a fresh understanding of community consciousness. Rather than suggest this insight in his written impression, he focuses on the ability of group dynamics to solve group problems. There is no doubt that group discussion will solve many problems, though it will only be able to do so when some of the more fundamental aspects of the

dynamic are released — cohesion, unity, and mutual understanding. From one point of view, this Brother and many persons like him have not experienced group growth on enough
occasions to be able to identify it clearly. Another Brother on
the same retreat appears to have a little better concept of community and was able to see this concept grow during the retreat.

> I tended to be very romantic in my ideals, looking and thinking
> I see things which aren't. My favorite antiphon is Thursday
> Vespers, "How good it is and how pleasant where brothers
> live in Unity." I have seen this at X for some time and am
> thankful that this retreat helped me realize it DOES exist.
> I also have been able to see how prejudiced I've been toward
> certain individuals and realize how much I'm really hurting
> myself. I know how offended I am when I'm not accepted
> for what I am and maybe now I'll be able to accept them
> as God made them. You've done something to X, Father,
> and we'll never be able to forget this experience and you.
> I hope some day our paths will cross again. Until that time,
> if ever, please remember we're all one and the same family.

By suggesting that he had already known something of
community consciousness through previous experience, this
Brother indirectly points out that he would be in a good position to experience growth in this dimension. A reflective reading
of his statement makes it easy to see that growth was a fact of
the experience. Not only does this Brother suggest that he experienced growth in the sense of community present, but also that
previous doubts concerning what community expression really
meant were allayed.

In pointing up the distinction between these two statements,
there is an attempt to suggest a personal conviction which has
grown during experience with groups. It has become clear over
the years that most persons have not experienced a sense of
community in their lives. Either there has been no such experience, or the experience is so meager that it has not impressed
them. From this vantage point, it is not surprising that one
would not express his experience in this area except in categories
already familiar. Common experience points to the fact that

such a tendency will stagnate groups on points which are largely difficulties in semantics. This points up the fact that there is a genuine void in the normal experience of community. From a natural and supernatural point of view, this vacuum in the experience of many can only be described as tragic.

In order to present a balanced approach to the personal statements of retreatants, it is important to focus also on the more specifically religious dimensions of the retreat. Though personal experience has made it difficult at times to understand the distinction made by many between the natural and supernatural impact of the retreat, many make the distinction and would attack the basis of the experience if the retreatants did not gain insight into prayer, love of Christ, and understanding of scripture as a result of the retreat. Such growth is always a part of the retreat which most clearly stands out, but it is not always clear that such expressions indicate the most significant growth in Christian principles.

Christ has pointed out that his basic law for attaining the kingdom of heaven is love of neighbor; and expressions which indicate growth in this area should, therefore, be more significant than any other. If a growth in understanding, compassion, and love for others were the only result such a retreat were able to effect, it would seem that the participants had genuinely grown to be better Christians. The final test which Christ uses to determine who will or will not enter into the kingdom with him is the love displayed toward others. This criterion is the one that dominates in the mind of Christ; it should also dominate ours.

Since the number of statements which center on the distinctly religious dimensions of the retreat always dominate, the question is largely irrelevant. As we will readily see during this part of the discussion retreatants are clearly aware of their spiritual growth, especially in their love of Christ. This is just one more indication that the goals of the classical retreat format are identical with those of the format based on group dynamics.

If there is anything heartening about these statements, it is the way they closely align the spiritual life with the world which surrounds them. There is a growing sense among Christians everywhere that religion has abstracted itself from the human condition. It is hoped that such statements indicate that this retreat format is a means of uniting the natural and supernatural in the way Christ obviously intended. Even a superficial reading of the gospel indicates that the Christian religion was never meant to exist except in relation to the needs of people. The very fact of the incarnation indicates in a dramatic manner the person-centered core upon which Christianity rests. Christ condemned unceasingly the ritualistic and legalistic minds of the Church in his time. There is little reason to doubt that the same would hold true in our day. If the retreat method suggested brings religion just a little closer to the person professing it, the effort will be rewarded.

When individuals speak of growth in Christ, discovery of Christ, or love of Christ without relating the person of Christ in some way to persons who surround them, one begins to wonder how much self-deception is involved in their concept. It is obvious that not every statement made concerning the person of Christ must be directly linked in some explicit manner, but the love of Christ in the gospel story must have both its foundation and culmination in others in order to be of genuine value. One Brother does not link directly search for the personality of Christ with the discovery of other persons, but it is obvious that the two are closely interwoven in his life.

> First of all, I want to thank you for this retreat. I benefited greatly from it. I think for the first time, I realized the value of reading and discussing the Bible, of really looking more closely for the personality of Christ. Secondly, I got to know more some people that have been in the house for some time. I learned or began to realize that I needed to understand others more and not to condemn them, but just their ideas if I didn't agree with them.

Our only source of knowledge about Christ and his message comes from the gospel which makes it important that we draw from this source in any attempts to know and understand him. In far too many efforts to encounter Christ, there is no genuine basis in scripture for much of the approach. A personally reflective understanding of the personality of Christ as revealed in the New Testament will alone make any attempts at dialogue for personal insight successful.

Rather than begin the difficult work of searching the gospel for a true picture of Christ, many would rather suggest the futility of future efforts because of previous failure in this area. The fact is that many speak as if they have a genuinely personal relationship with Christ without the concurrent insight into scripture. For the vast majority of persons, such an approach is exceedingly unrealistic.

Once exposed to the excitement and challenge of personal involvement in scripture, many make such an approach a permanent part of their lives. A firm foundation for the use of such phrases as encounter with Christ and love of Christ will produce real insights when one draws closer to the personality Christ displayed to us through the New Testament. The first glimpse into the person of Christ can be a thrilling experience. One Sister found it so fulfilling that she feared that the experience would not stay with her.

> I came to this retreat excited about the newness of it — but, after the model discussion, I almost decided that it would be a very difficult thing for me. Also, I had deep prejudices about the sub-group to which I was assigned and its leader. Worst of all, I dreaded having to look for Christ in the Gospels when for so many years I had failed to do so — (after honest effort, too!)

> It's almost over, and I hate for it to be, because I did find out how to find Christ in the Gospels. Still, it seems too good to be true and I dread that I'll go back to "every day" and not be able to keep Him. Also, I discovered "other people" in my sub-group and became friends with the leader. I didn't imagine there was so much to people; that they are so beautiful and good . . .

> I can't explain in words — but I know what the Spirit is who is in this group and the knowledge makes me glad. There's much more. It will take a lifetime for it to jell and I like looking forward to it.

We find the many elements of scriptural quest in this statement. In her honesty concerning early negative reactions in the
search for Christ in the gospel, Sister reveals a reaction common
to many. Despite what seemed honest efforts to encounter the
Christ of the gospel, a certain negative reaction was recognized
which had undoubtedly grown for some time. Coupled with
this negative reaction was another which created some misgivings
about some of the individuals in the group within which she
was to attempt this search. The end of the retreat finds her,
however, with completely new ideas concerning her own ability
to "find Christ in the gospels" as well as fresh insights into
other persons. One gains the impression, from the wording of the
statement, that the two developments were very much dependent
on each other.

Many merely suggest their growth in understanding Christ
is related to their insights and understanding of others, but some
are able to be more specific about the relationship. Since often
those attempting to grow in the love of Christ are explicit about
the fact that their insights are giving them a completely new
understanding of what this love means, it is not surprising to
discover a certain lack of definition in their statements. Rather
than giving a completely new approach to their own spirituality,
some feel the experience allowed them to enrich already existing
attitudes. It is not unusual to discover greater insight into the
relation between love of Christ and love of neighbor in such a
person.

Certainly, one of the most obvious outcomes for me is a
greater love and attraction and appreciation for God's Word
in the Gospel. I feel that Christ became even more alive to
me than I felt he already was and I have been favored, I
suppose one would say, to have felt his real presence to me
and with me for some time almost without ceasing. This has
come about through my love for people and their love for
me. It is hard to describe what was present in our small
group — it was a tremendous experience. From the various
comments, ours must have been the most exciting for it was
terribly open and honest and most personal. I know that
when I was relating a certain matter about myself I very

definitely felt a strong drawing of the others to me. It has deepened an already present conviction of mine about the person and that we must get involved . . . As far as I am concerned, I know that I drew even closer to all people, deepened already existing friendships, and even beyond to the people on the "outside." But in a sense, this has never been a real problem to me for the person has always meant so much to me. It was a real joy to know you personally, to know Christ more personally and all the other persons around. I think it is a tremendous beginning.

We see here highlighted many aspects of the goals sought by the retreat dynamics. The basic value at the core of the statement, however, was the linkage between growth in interpersonal relations and the sense of Christ's presence. Through the openness and understanding displayed toward others, each individual grows in his awareness of Christ and the gospel message. A rich insight into the gospel makes understanding and compassion for others that much more possible. The greater involvement with others also allows one to probe new depth in the New Testament message.

Just as the dynamic between persons on a retreat is normally released in stages which can be clearly distinguished, it appears that there is also a similar process which occurs within persons attempting to encounter Christ. In its first stage, the person takes an honest look at himself and discovers a need. Honesty growing within any given individual allows him to begin to separate his true identity from that one he has attempted to create in order to satisfy unconscious needs. Though individuals might use different terminology to suggest the personal impact such a revelation might have for them, this self-awareness is really no different from that suggested by great philosophical minds throughout the ages.

Modern psychology indicates that most of us create an image of ourselves to the extent that unfulfilled needs remain beneath our personal makeup. With an insight into the dichotomy between our true and idealized concepts, we are left with the need for help. Under such a state of stress, many recognize the need for a personal contact with the Christ who can heal the wounds and teach the way to a greater sense of fulfillment and humanity than was previously present. Through the words of one seminarian novice, we get some insight into how an individual might come to understand such dynamics.

> This retreat has, in a sense, been more beneficial to me than any other retreat because for the first time I really took an honest evaluation of what I *really* am, rather than what I hoped and made myself believe that I was. It, in a very true sense, has been shocking — but then we can't really face life maturely without FRANKLY knowing ourselves. It also has made me aware of the need for Christ in each of us, for only then can we find fulfillment — real maturity of life!

In this stage of purification, there is a great deal of pain obvious because of the "shocking" nature of what is revealed. In order to cope with such honesty about self, one must necessarily endure a great deal of ambiguity. A great deal of effort has been spent in maintaining this false ideal and the experience of seeing it disappear will obviously involve emotional upheaval.

In moving out from this base of self-understanding to deeper awareness, it is not so obvious that the path must be also filled with pain. The fact is that each movement forward means a further chipping away at the ideal self one has constructed. To further confuse the issue, one only moves positively through the suffering implicit in personal growth when he is in an atmosphere which places him at ease with his own emotions. From the base of a calm and tension-free atmosphere, the individual can have the physical reserve and necessary perspective to grow closer to the ideal Christ has placed before us. The stage of development which follows the shock of self-realization is described well by a student after his experience.

> I am more relaxed, I can reflect better and I have a great desire to continue this openness, honesty, and participation as a form of life with others. I have discovered more Christ, the significance of life and its fulfillment. I have sensed that happiness that comes when you are at peace with the heart. I have suffered. This I regard as part of my development

and not as a harm. It relieved a tension of fear of what is
to come.

As is implied in any form of growth, there is much fear and
pain in attempting to follow the gospel message to attain a
fundamental Christlike attitude. In attempting to release the
Christian principles of compassion, understanding, and love,
each person must take personal risks which involve overcoming
personal fears and imply a basic trust in others. Every step involved in becoming more aware of Christ in daily life will be
taken only with the greatest caution and at the expense of
personal security.

If the growth is to reach out even further than personal
discovery of Christ in one's life, then the vision of all united
in Christ must become part of the growth process. It becomes
difficult in such a stage of development to distinguish one's concept of Christ personally present through inner promptings and
the presence he manifests when the individual is in communion
with others. Though such presence is really no different in the
two cases, there is a difference in degree. This difference might
be best expressed in terms of the greater intensity which manifests
itself when there is a community expression of Christ's love.

> During the last five years of my life, I have become more and
> more aware of Christ within my life. Such presence became
> increasingly obvious due to the calm and relaxed attitude that
> came upon me in my dealings with others. In some mysterious
> way, I was able to give help to many people — some des-
> perately in need of that same help. In so many ways, I was
> aware that I was really not doing anything concrete to help
> these people. Despite my sense of inadequacy, more were
> seeking aid and comfort from me. It was during those periods
> that I began to become aware of this vague presence which
> I could only identify with Christ somehow growing within me.
> Now I am mysteriously confused. After this retreat I begin
> to become aware of a new presence. Not really anything new
> in the sense of different; but rather new because of the
> greater intensity manifested. I hardly even dare talk of it
> for fear it will somehow be destroyed in the process. I will
> only say that the manifestations have produced a wonderful

internal freedom and joy which make me look to the future with a true sense of excitement and wonder.

In the emphasis given here and in the actual experience, growth in the knowledge and love of Christ are central to the goals and results of the retreat. If we consider any other aspect of the results, it will only be as a secondary result of this primary emphasis. Such secondary results must be placed in proper perspective but there is no doubt concerning their value in themselves and as evidence that the growth in the primary goal was not illusionary.

One of the most frequently mentioned aids to overall religious development is the greater value prayer achieves in the individual as a result of the retreat. Within the context of many statements, this greater ease and joy through prayer manifests itself in many ways. As a result of the new dimension revealed, many find a means to pass over a period of aridity in prayer while others are able to reach new depths in a prayer life which is progressing well. In one Sister's statement, she manifests the joy in discovering a sense of community in the prayer life which has been in progress.

The retreat was good for me in that I was able to add a real sense of community and pride in it to the prayer life I have begun to develop through the year. I felt I gave of myself and received from others that sort of charity which I consider to be the foundation of the religious life. I hope that the day of worshiping monads in this community has passed.

It could be considered as part of the previously mentioned ability the experience gives to persons which allows them to gain perspective on themselves, but there is a special religious dimension to the choice of a vocation. In working with seminarians, in particular, there was strong evidence that the retreat gave them the kind of perspective on their vocational decision which had been previously impossible. The growth of a religious depends to a great extent on his ability to be at peace with himself in a moving toward a decision which will be the basis of his life. Such a decision moves into the special category of aids to religious development which are more than the normal secondary considerations. In the words of one novice, such new insights into the question of vocation will enable him "to make a decision more intelligently than before."

> I believe this retreat was good for me because it forced me to question many things that I had previously assumed. This questioning has added insight to a decision on my vocation. Although this retreat and some aspects of the novitiate have given me doubts as to my place in the community and even in the priesthood, I am glad that these things have come to light now when I have a year to consider them. I am tired and confused now but I feel that from this jolt out of security, I will be able to make a decision more intelligently than before. This has undoubtedly been the best retreat I have ever attended. It forced me to become active and practical. The mystery and false holiness of the old-style retreat were absent and an all important honesty was present to me.

The special atmosphere created on the retreat causes individuals to experience a special kind of concern toward the end of the period. When the end is in sight and retreatants begin to realize they are soon to return to their usual routine, there is a fear which begins to build within. Though in their reflective moments they know the fear is the same kind of fear that the beginning of the retreat provoked, they cannot help but feel frightened at the prospect of carrying this kind of experience into the drudgery of normal existence. One Brother expressed his doubts ambivalently.

> This retreat has been an experience. "What has been accomplished?"; "How different am I now as opposed to before the retreat?"; are questions that still cannot be answered as far as I am concerned. I think I am capable of understanding my Brothers more and yet I worry that we as a house will slip back into our old ways which have plagued us greatly in the past. I think the answer to "Was this retreat good or bad?" will be answered by this house in the ensuing months. Personally, my love for others has, I feel, grown. I must now keep the principles of the retreat, toleration, Christ as he is in the gospels, and love, ever before me in meditation, reflec-

tion, and prayer. Due to the relaxed attitude of this retreat
I would say that I prefer it to the old type of conference-
vegitate retreats. This retreat has been quite an experience
and I just hope I can remember it, in essence, the rest of
my life.

Because he can remember past examples of conflict within
the house, the Brother naturally wonders if this will not become
the rule again when the special effects of the retreat wear off.
He sees the house can exist in a genuine spirit of community
and undoubtedly wants to do what he can to continue this
spirit. Somehow he knows that the same fears and doubts
plaguing him also concern all the other members of the house.
If everyone begins to retreat into former patterns, who will have
the courage to move against the tide? His basic question was
repeated by a Sister on another retreat.

I have mixed emotions. I feel that if we Religious could live
in the climate created by this retreat (openness, communication, etc.), we might approach the real meaning of community
life. We could experience one another's support. But I am
saddened, I am discouraged because I do not feel that it is
a possible situation for a whole year. I am afraid that all too
soon we will fall back in the old "coverup."

But a little hope is that with the warmth and understanding
of some people — such as I have experienced from you —
I may be able to "overcome."

Since all realize that special aids were introduced into the
retreat in order to create the atmosphere, there is a fear that
without such support the intensity cannot be sustained. The
further realization that such interpersonal qualities develop only
through the interest and sacrifice of everyone involved causes
such a fear to become more intense. With these realities clearly
in mind, few can have the kind of optimism that one student
displayed.

This retreat has been one of the most fruitful experiences I
have ever had. Its benefits will not have been exhausted

just in the days here but rather the whole outlook and attitude which it provided will be of great value and assistance throughout life. You were personally magnificent in your direction; and in all sincerity, it has been a week I will never forget.

In many ways, both views of the retreat are correct. Since the special atmosphere is bound to be eradicated in many of its more obvious extrinsic characteristics, the burden on each person to recapture some of its impact is going to be much greater. No matter how many factors affect the individual attempting to comprehend some of the internal values he discovered during the retreat, he can never forget the experience. Even though he might attempt to rationalize about the retreat in order to excuse himself from re-creating the interpersonal experiences within his life, there always remains an awareness of what did happen and what it meant for himself and others. The impact of the retreat carries no further than this basic awareness in the future but the value of the experience does endure.

In order to end this discussion on the most promising note possible, it would seem that nothing would be more satisfying than addressing ourselves to the potential the retreat holds for introducing renewal into religious communities. Renewal has come to stand for splits between individuals and groups in far too many communities. Rather than stimulate a deeper and richer love between members of the community, the attempts to renew community structure create a sense of hostility and anger. To the extent that attempts to renew community life create discord between the members, one questions the value of the attempt.

All are guilty of focusing on the external forms of renewal and escaping the real dimension of such change. If individuals argue concerning the value of saying certain prayers in private or common, for example, there is little hope that the issue of prayer's actual value will ever be ascertained. As long as the most important issues concern external ritualism, arguments will never reach the level of dialogue. Under such a cloud, renewal can never mean any more than individual decisions concerning which form of ritual should be followed.

The attempt of the retreat is to reverse the tendency to discuss externals and focus on internal attitudes and reactions. It is possible to solve differences without even touching externals directly. Since the real conflict lies within the person's own self concept, arguments concerning the individual's "reasons" for opposing a given change are doomed to failure. If we take a moment to see the conflict from the standpoint of an "older Sister," some insight into the real dimensions of the problem will be illuminated.

> I feel that the Retreat taught me much about communicating with others. As an older religious I thought that a discussion must have an "authority" guide. The young and their interest in words and abstract (conditions or problems)? I understand better. I can see that their background does not prepare them to see what renewal means to older Sisters — a reconstruction of thought and attitudes. For example the spiritual reading in the last fifty years had gradually changed until perhaps, ten years ago — then Bang! Bewildered we read and prayed — I found in the discussions that I had "renewed" rather well, and that they will be helpful for others still confused if I help. For a fearful creature it has been a peaceful retreat for me.

It is the attitude displayed by this particular Sister which will press religious toward genuine growth in the framework of their community life. In her statement we see a complexity of factors which have given her an entirely new outlook on herself and the other members of her community. At the outset, she admits to an attitude concerning discussion which she now questions. The "authority" guide is not necessary for a valuable discussion. On a much richer level she has begun to see that there is no dishonesty in the younger Sister's failure to understand "what renewal means to older Sisters." Her final plea to be understood herself reveals a real note of the genuine and and honest.

This was the impact of the retreat as reflected in some of the many statements collected over the years. In reading them again, personal reactions were strong. From many statements of personal conflict and resolution, many of the retreat experiences were recalled with a great deal of satisfaction. Simply stated, it can be said that none of the statements begin to point to the personal satisfaction, insight and growth which result from leading so many different groups in the process of self-discovery. In his final statement, one student saw something of the satisfaction which is part of the leader's reward.

> Until this final point in the retreat, I have been involved in the meaning this experience has had for me. Though I was prepared to address myself to this, I suddenly realized that you have been involved in this way with many groups over a long period of time. My present reaction is akin to envy. If I have gained so much from just this one exposure to other persons, what must be your reward for having shared so much with others in such a meaningful manner. I originally wanted to thank you for giving so much to us and now realize that such statements would be meaningless compared to the impact of the experience. In spite of this, I want to say thanks and hope you will realize what I mean by it.

9.   the human retreat master

Since most of the discussion has focused on the ideal retreat, it is only fair to discuss the many barriers which could hinder the actualization of this model concept. Human weaknesses will always block the path to the ideal community experience. Whether the barriers manifest themselves in the leader or the retreatants, there is a great deal of human frailty which stands between any group and the ideal group experience.

Since the leader is crucial in developing within any group the growth it seeks, this discussion will concentrate on his potential weaknesses in stimulating such growth. It might be suggested that all of the human frailties to be discussed could just as easily be applied to the retreatants. Since the group turns to him for aid in creating a community, however, it is reasonable to look to the leader's possible shortcomings in predicting impediments to success.

In discussing the normal repetitive shortcomings and failures of the leader, we must take for granted that we are speaking of one who is earnestly attempting to use the dynamic effectively. It is obvious that anyone unconvinced of the value such a retreat format offers will fail in its application. Nothing could be more futile than a person attempting to apply the retreat dynamic with serious misgivings concerning its use.

The purpose of this discussion is to point out the human weaknesses that even the enthusiastic leader can expect will hinder his success. As experience with the approach increases, one can normally recognize these shortcomings within himself. Because such recognition is normally the first step in eliminating such failings, the retreat master will become more and more effective in reaching the ideal of the retreat experience as he learns to accept himself in his weaknesses as well as his strengths.

Since there is a great deal of difference between the approach of any two retreat masters, the discussion will be directed to weaknesses most individuals will encounter in attempting to create an atmosphere conducive to an effective retreat experience. The retreat method is hindered to the extent that he is not coping with his own inadequacies. For the retreat master attempting to work within the context of group discussion, however, such weaknesses will be more obvious and all the more destructive if they are not handled on the conscious level.

All that can be asked of any retreat master is that he be honest with himself. If personal pride does not block him from recognizing the simple fact that he is similar to the vast majority of people in his personality defects, he will be able to move to a more effective relationship with the retreatants and thereby aid them in their struggles. From this firm foundation, he will need little more than experience in moving effectively toward the goal of creating the ideal retreat asmosphere.

FEELINGS OF INADEQUACY

It may seem strange to suggest that the first thing a retreat master must come to grips with is his personal feelings of inadequacy. Though some will not readily admit to having such feelings, there is little doubt that nearly all have some sense of personal inadequacy. The irony of the situation is that the reason most people will not admit their true feelings in this regard is that they do not recognize such a feeling as normal or natural.

Just as these personal feelings of inadequacy might lead group members to remain silent during discussion, the same kind of feelings can reduce the leader's effectiveness in creating a freedom to participate. Once the member senses a fear in the leader, he is undoubtedly going to be reinforced in his own fear of opening himself up to others. It is only reasonable that no leader can give to others something which he does not possess himself.

The leader is certainly the most vulnerable member of the group. Under normal circumstances, he must be the first one to open himself to others. Coupling this fact with the obvious reality that he is normally expected to tell the group how they are to perform during the period of retreat, the leader will be in a position to be attacked by members at any time. It is therefore not uncommon to hear threatening statements such as the following:

"We came to this retreat to hear you, not each other."

"We need someone to let us know when we are clearly wrong."

"I'm sick and tired of these discussions."

Under such circumstances, it would not be surprising at all to see the leader react defensively. The pressure of the moment may bring feelings of inadequacy to the surface and tend to force the leader to become defensive in his manner. Any group at all perceptive will sense this reaction and become less likely themselves to react honestly in the same situation. Though most of the dynamics present in this situation are beneath the surface, they are more real than any word or action which is overtly performed.

Though they are only able to admit it in a moment of reflectivity, most leaders feel their own inadequacies in their attempts to lead a retreat based on group dynamics. Many times during the retreat, participants will turn to them to "do something" about one crisis or another. If there is anything which is opposed to the entire concept of group dynamics, however, it is the leader who forces himself upon a situation in order to ease a particular crisis.

When a person's self-concept is threatened, he often becomes aggressive and hostile towards the person attempting to probe. Ironically, when an individual is attacked directly or indirectly at the personal level, he is likely to retaliate by questioning the worth of the person attacking. By some form of logic that is only understood at the emotional level, we not uncommonly attempt to elevate our own self-esteem by aggression toward others.

If the leader retaliates against the individual who has assaulted him, he will undoubtedly create a fear of being honest among others within the group. There is no doubt that such fear will be felt by others and reinforce the already complex fears which trap them in isolation from one another. Experience and scientific studies both point to the fact that the members of the group will emulate the leader in his strengths and weaknesses. If the leader loses control of his inadequate feelings before the group, there is little doubt that the retreatants will, in turn, become more conscious of their own.

Since persons do not want others to discover their personal weaknesses, they will normally reveal such weaknesses as subtly as possible. If a retreat master were to directly retaliate against aggression, for example, he would obviously be open to criticism and exposed in his weakness. A much more skillful manner of rebuke would be to question the worth of the retreatants generally. It would be difficult, for example, for the retreatants to criticize the retreat master for telling them what they must think if they are to make profitable use of the retreat period. Since his role is one which allows group domination, the best rebuke available would be for him to return to that role.

Insofar as the retreat master allows himself to return to a position of power over the group, it is that much less likely that the retreatants will be able to discover themselves in the experience. Rather than move along the painful path toward an interpersonal awareness of one another, it is easier to play the docile role normally expected of them. Especially when that passive role tendency is reinforced by the mood, actions, or words of the leader, the hope of unleashing dynamics within the group is minimized.

In order for the retreat master to be in command of himself in such situations, it is important that he concentrate his attention on the present moment. While it is impossible for him to completely escape such emotional realities as his own feelings of inadequacy, he will be able to place them in proper context by focusing his attention on the situation at hand. To the extent that such emotional expression is present, he must, of course, be aware of it. The danger is to attempt to direct his attention elsewhere or escape from such emotion. Hiding from himself in the situation will undoubtedly create a greater danger of being disruptive to the atmosphere he is attempting to generate.

Though we have not attempted to describe the possible causes for such feelings of inadequacy, it might be said that they are a normal part of life. The individual who does not experience such feelings is certainly the exception rather than the rule. Reality is the ability to accept and express such feelings rather than to escape from them. With such an approach to the emotions, the individual is able to grow and permit others the same potential growth which must be the rationale for the retreat experience.

RESPONSIBILITY

If there is any one emotion which constantly bothers the individual attempting to implement a group-centered approach to retreats, it is his feelings of responsibility. Though one never completely escapes such an emotion, it is in early experiences with the approach that the retreat master will normally have the greatest struggles in this area. Not only does the leader have this strong sense that he is responsible for the outcome of the retreat but others will be constantly reminding him of the role he should be playing. It is no easy task to withstand this internal and external pressure.

The responsibility the leader speaks of is normally a rather general feeling within himself. He often attempts to identify it, however, in some concrete way. Some retreat masters will express this feeling by building the discussion for fear the group will reach the "wrong" goals. There are those times during the retreat when it is obvious that the group is changing its attitudes toward many things and it is not certain what the final attitude will be. During such a change it is normal for the retreat master to feel a compulsion to enter the discussion in such a way that the "right" conclusions will be reached. As can be easily seen, it would not be difficult to suggest numerous situations in which the retreat master might feel the weight of responsibility.

While there is no doubt about the reality of such a tendency to feel responsible, there is a need to place this tendency in its proper perspective. Before understanding such a need, one must reflectively consider the nature of this responsibility he feels. He might profitably question the direction and nature of the feelings which cause him so much conflict. One only begins to come to grips with such feelings when he honestly reflects on questions such as the following:

"Do I really know the correct goals and answers which this group is earnestly seeking?"

"Am I really to presume responsibility for their development?"

"Am I a better judge than the group of the spiritual needs which are most pertinent to this group?"

"Am I more concerned with my need to help than I am with their conflict?"

THE NEED TO CHANGE OTHERS

Whether he realizes it or not, the leader's tendency to feel responsible for the group depends largely upon how much he experiences a need to change the group. This need, of course, is very much tied to his doubts concerning the group's ability to act responsibly in an atmosphere of freedom. These weaknesses in the leader's ability to place responsibility into the hands of the group will be expressed in the subtlest manner, but this in no way reflects the strength of the leader's feelings. Even in the leader who is not conscious of any such desire, there may be an overpowering drive which will not permit him to allow others to choose their own direction in discussion.

It is reasonable to be concerned, for example, about the possibility that the group will not accept their responsibility and blame the leader for the failure of the retreat. The only way to finally reply to such a concern is by pointing to experience. When groups say they have actually sensed that they were being given genuine freedom and responsibility, they have responded by accepting this charge and using it constructively. When leaders show a good deal of reluctance to trust the group, on the other hand, the group normally fails to meet this obligation.

There are many who are extremely disconcerted when they discover such apparently unbounded faith in the ability of a group. They point out that past experience demonstrates the destructive tendencies which will be released in an atmosphere. It would certainly be dishonest not to admit that many groups may not cope with the weight of responsible decision due to their lack of insight, education, intelligence, or apathy. And it would be only right to admit that such objections are genuine and create ambivalence in all leaders.

The group-centered leader, on the other hand, knows that many groups have difficulty breaking the habit of relying on the leader for direction and find a new outlook difficult to accept. Coupling this with the fact that many leaders claiming to give responsibility to groups are actually only placing a limited trust with the members of the group, it is not surprising to find that many groups fail. Experience points clearly to the fact that the process is slow in both the leader and the group. Consequently, it is not surprising that the group-centered leader accepts the fact that many failures in the approach will not destroy his faith in the process.

When all the arguments have ceased, the retreat master with experience and faith in the retreat dynamic can finally only say that the group will accept responsibility when given the implicit trust of the leader. The attempt to logically prove, one way or another, the success or failure of such an approach will ultimately fail. This is not surprising, however, when one realizes that the basis of the argument lies not in the intellect, but rather in the emotions.

It might be comforting for some to realize that this feeling of responsibility is not limited to the beginner. Even the most experienced group leader finds his conscience afflicting him at times. When one realizes that there are always periods in any group experience during which no positive progress is apparent,

it should not be startling to accept the fact that guilt feelings
bother the mature as well as the novice leader. The only difference is that the effective leader will be able to sustain his
trust in the group more effectively during these difficult periods.

TAKING CHARGE

Initially one might not expect a fear of rejection would cause
a leader to avoid the democratic process. It would seem that
as an "authority guide" the retreat master would leave himself
more vulnerable to criticism and rejection. Because he is attempting to instruct others in the best way of approaching the
spiritual life, however, the retreat master who "takes charge"
is multiplying the number of objections which the retreatants
may raise. It appears on the surface that such a retreat master
is more open to criticism than one who merely leads the discussion.

To look at the same argument from another point of view,
the group-centered leader has protected himself from any attack
by suggesting that the group itself supply their own direction.
If the retreat proves a failure, he need only point to the fact
that he had placed the goals and means to those goals in the
hands of the group. If there were any failure the group itself
must be responsible for it. Any fear of rejection would appear
to be readily handled and the retreat master's self-concept
remain intact.

After a little reflection, however, it becomes apparent that
the retreat master who puts himself in a position as an "authority
guide" will not be easily vulnerable to attack. In order for
anyone to question a retreat master who has assumed the
authority role, he must normally speak without knowing whether
he has any support from others present. In the silence and
monologue of the normal retreat, it would be difficult to take
such a chance.

There is truth in the statement that the retreat master in
his lectures gives retreatants much more to criticize than he
would in leading a discussion. All participants will necessarily
make some kind of judgment on the leader's talks. No matter

what kind of format is proposed for the retreat, a great many judgments will be made by the retreatants. The great difference between the monologue and dialogue retreats, however, is the fact that the former does not have any real means for expressing praise or rejection of such feelings.

Since the retreat dynamics is based on generating communication between members, the retreat master who uses this approach leaves himself vulnerable to criticism. By attempting to create a free atmosphere for exchange, he is encouraging all with either praise or blame to express such feeling. The more freedom one is offered to communicate his concerns, the more likely he will be to express his rejection of the retreat master.

FEAR OF REJECTION

Since only the most stable persons are able to distinguish between a rejection of themselves and a rejection of their ideas, the fear of rejection will undoubtedly be a permanent part of the life of the retreat master who attempts the discussion retreat. As with all temperamental obstructions to the effective group atmosphere, the most important growth will occur in the retreat master when he becomes aware of such weaknesses. Individuals who are aware they operate in certain ways when they feel rejected have begun the major work of discovering the real dimensions of these feelings.

For the immediate future, fear of rejection remains a dominant factor in our society. Whether we look to education, industry, or government, we see that our society is stimulated by the fear of rejection. The child is "educated" to fear negative evaluation. The worker produces under the shadow of those in authority. A great deal of the measured progress in society is stimulated by this basic fear of rejection.

To say that the retreat master is going to have a basic fear of rejection is to say that he is a member of our society. The reason for highlighting this fear is that his work is to create an atmosphere which will leave him more vulnerable than he would be in the ordinary course of events. In order to continue along this path, he should be more aware than most people of his feelings in this matter. Otherwise, he will be in danger of being overcome by a force primarily because he is unable to define it.

In order to escape this fear of rejection, people will use any number of personal mannerisms to defend themselves from such attack. While it has never been determined whether such a need to defend ourselves develops as a result of heredity and environment or whether it is instinctive in the organism, it appears to apply to all men. When challenged concerning an idea about which they feel strongly, for example, many will become immediately aggressive toward their adversary without reflecting even momentarily on the dimensions of the challenge. One can easily see the self-defeating nature of such a defense as more aggression merely increases the need to defend.

Many find it necessary to establish certain false premises about themselves and the world in which they live in order to escape some of the pain and suffering implicit in that same world. Some part of their world then is constructed rather than discovered through experience. Someone disturbing this construct by suggesting that it has not developed from common experience is touching a vulnerable spot and the accused will spend a great deal of psychic energy in order to preserve the false premises of his life. When one realizes that the average individual may have woven a complex network of beliefs, attitudes, values, and actions around some of the false prejudices he developed early, it is not surprising that he would hesitate to change any part of the pattern for fear the entire structure might collapse.

The tendency to resist change under pressure is the one temperamental factor most likely to be disruptive to communication. The importance of recognizing such a factor at work in any group discussion is obvious to even the most unskilled observer. If the disagreements which naturally occur develop to the point where someone must change his opinion in order to end such disagreement, a real permanent disruption in communication may occur. The leader must necessarily become skilled in recognizing such disruptive tendencies early and labor with the participants to enable them to work through the conflict in order that the lines of communication will not be severed completely.

If it is important for the leader to be sensitive to any challenges developing between group members, it is vital that he personally not create even the most subtle rebuke. Since there will be many occasions during which the group hostility will be directed toward the leader rather than at its proper object, the leader must be extremely sensitive to any tendency to react in defense of false premises upon which his own value system is built. The group naturally looks to the leader to epitomize a Christian attitude toward everyone. Receiving even a hint of a rebuke from the retreat master can create a reluctance in the individual and in the group to begin honest communication.

The group will be extremely aware of and tend to imitate what they discover in the retreat master's personality. This puts a heavy burden on the person of the retreat master and he is obliged to develop greater and greater awareness of himself in order to be of utmost aid in helping others to grow beyond their present stage of maturity. In areas which may be particularly difficult for retreatants to discuss, there is a need for special effort. The retreat master who reinforces the tendency to defend by his own actions is creating unnecessary obstacles to group development.

ACCEPTANCE

Continuing to reveal the complicated tasks which lie before the group leader, we might stress the acceptance the leader must convey to the members who will tend to reject him. All should be able to appreciate the difficulty involved in generating warmth toward one who has created a tense and threatening atmosphere by his words or actions. The skilled leader with a great deal of experience will still discover himself slipping into very subtle forms of rejection as his own self-concept is threatened. Many of these forms of rejection are all the more dangerous because of their subtle nature. The forms of attack which are not identified as such may easily leave the recipient in a state of fear. Such fear can clearly be all the more destructive due to its undefined nature.

In order to illustrate this somewhat, we might turn to a concrete example of subtle attack in the face of rejection. A retreat master who has been attacked for not having enough courage to speak out for what he considers truth might readily find such attack a threat to his self-concept. Rather than recognize it as such, however, he could more comfortably reflect on the need to change the attitudes of the person leveling the attack. Through indirect attempts to change the other person, the retreat master may preserve his own self-esteem and not appear to be returning the attack.

This need to change others may be expressed in a manner so subtle as to appear perfectly normal and even accepting. A leader is able to discourage behavior that makes him uncomfortable by merely questioning certain kinds of statements. Consider, for example, how even the most apparently genuine responses might readily be used to change others.

Have you reflected carefully on that statement?

Would you say that is an honest expression of the way you feel?

Do you honestly believe that is correct?

On what authority do you make such a statement?

We are not generally aware of the impact such judgments have upon others. We would more readily understand the reaction of others by reflecting on the impact this sort of rejection might have upon ourselves in similar situations. Since the shame experience is heightened in a group setting, it is all the more important that such subtle rejections be eliminated. Experience in groups shows that individuals may completely withdraw when exposed to such attack and, even more dangerous to the group, turn the attack on others even more vigorously and destructively.

LOCUS OF EVALUATION

Another danger implicit in the expressed need to change others on the part of the leader is the tendency within the group to return to the leader as the locus of evaluation. We have previously discussed the necessity for diffusing leadership among the members of the group and the tendency for the members to reject any such responsibility. Any return to the desire of the group to have the leader assume the responsibility will be difficult to eliminate. One might note that even positive evaluations have the same tendency to turn responsibility away from the members and toward the leader. Whether positive or negative needs to establish a certain kind of person within the context of the group is operating, there is a tendency in the leader to see a behavior emerge which fulfills his expectations. It is difficult to allow each individual emerge as he honestly views himself at any given time. When the need to change others is expressed in even the subtlest manner, there is a serious possibility that the more profound goals of the retreat may be seriously damaged.

If the need to change the group is expressed clearly enough, the leader may easily create a group which finds its unity in its common reaction against authority. The leader may place himself outside of the group by permitting members to transfer their reaction against authority, generally, to him specifically. Some of the danger in allowing such freedom lies in the fact that the retreat master no longer will have any effect on the group. The far greater danger is the possibility that the retreatants will tend to reject even his positive and creative contributions.

In this frame of reference, the retreatants will tend to be stimulated by their reaction against the "authority" of the retreat master rather than in positive reaction to the needs of the group. Even at the expense of truth and honesty, statements will be made to counter the expressions of the leader. As a result of such a situation, the leader becomes leader in name only with even his membership in the group expressed nominally.

In the average childhood experience, there is little opportunity for the individual to test his own perceptions and experiences. He is rather "trained" from an early age to rely on an "authority." The childlike awe of the world around is normally destroyed by parents who do not want to permit even the slightest degree of wonder to persist. It is as if the genuine philosophical inquiry which is so normal and natural to the child is actually a threat to the adult who quickly supplies ready-made half truths in order to end a disconcerting questioning process. If parents were a little more honest about their own confusion, children might have a greater chance to open new frontiers of knowledge. Rather than allow such a confusion to persist, however, we readily supply information and with it an automatic response to authority.

It is genuinely understandable, then, that the retreat master will necessarily have to be aware of the fact that any attempt to destroy the authority guide will be met with resistance. Without the ability to be submissive or hostile to authority one must rely upon himself as the locus of evaluation. Such a reality may be terribly frightening when we realize that there has been nothing like this in one's previous experience. More than recognizing and tolerating the reactions of others to his role as authority guide, the leader must be even more aware of his own tendencies to assume the leadership role too readily.

If the childhood experience trains the child to expect authority to end his questioning process, it also produces an increasing desire within the child to be able to assume the authority role himself. We can experience the interwoven tendencies to be both submissive and hostile to authority and the reflective person can see the connection between the desire to lead and be led. If past experience forces the leader to release his tendency to dominate, the retreat experience may readily be destroyed. As we have seen in our discussion of the drive to change others, the tendency to dominate may be expressed in the most subtle manner. The attempt to express the drive subtly will not only fail to eliminate its destructive power, however, but even to increase its crippling impact.

PLANNING

If we were looking for a thermometer to indicate how much we are dominated by our tendency to be authoritative, we could readily examine our need to organize and plan. We look to business, industry, military, or even education and find generally the stereotype of leadership which emphasizes the ability to plan. It is as if the leader's strategy were his most important asset. Since the paradigm for leadership emphasizes the leader's skill in organizing and planning, some discussion about this skill might be in order.

There is little or no doubt that leadership training emphasizes the skill and knowledge necessary to lead others. Whether we look at the basic principles taught in leadership training or the foundation upon which promotions are based, industry, military, and other organizations appear to look fundamentally for skill and knowledge. The ideals of leadership are usually those found in the well-educated individual who has the patience to acquire all of the facts before organizing them into a balanced plan of action. With his approach clearly in his mind, he then skillfully influences others to accept his plan as the correct approach to the problem.

The only thing about the strategy approach to leadership which might encourage reflection is the fact that it is basically manipulative. Rather than drawing on the resources implicit within the given group, it instructs them by persuasion to an approach which may not hold any significance. To the extent that any leader relies on superior knowledge and astute ability to persuade, he will be likely to leave doubts and even opposition within the ranks of the subordinates upon whom he must rely to carry out his task.

If one is to shift the emphasis in leadership from knowledge and skill, a question suddenly arises. In what does the essential concept of leadership consist? The answer to such a question is not easy. Even when the answer is suggested to the most open-minded, a period of experience with the implications of such an approach to leadership must evolve before one may honestly determine whether this approach is genuinely realistic.

There is no doubt that some organizational preparation is necessary in the retreat. Though the most unstructured leader will concern himself with some planning for the retreat, there is no reason to eliminate the possibility of the group determining all details including the time and place of meetings as well as size and composition of groups. With all or even most of the normal planning being eliminated, the question of leader preparation becomes obscure. A common reaction to the uncertainty created is a great concern over the use of a period for preparation. Just how does one prepare himself for such an approach?

It is not difficult to realize that the preparation for such an experience must basically consist in attitude training. Whether it consists in us becoming aware of our own lack of faith in others or our fear of hostility, we must become consciously sensitive to our underlying attitudes. By pursuing this thought through to its logical conclusion, it is evident that preparation for such a retreat must focus on the person of the leader rather than some subject matter external to him. The obvious implication is that immediate preparation is necessarily limited. Though something in the way of reflective consideration of attitudes alone or with other leaders will be the best preparation for the leader, the real goal of leadership will only be achieved by maintaining a constant state of self-awareness. The leader grows in effectiveness only when he is constantly aware of his need to develop daily and is successful when he attains the proper attitude toward himself and others. To expect a major development along this line in a short period of time is just unrealistic. The kind of long-range plan to affect personal attitudes must be a life project.

TOLERANCE LEVEL

It is clear that the tolerance level of the leader must be high in order to effectively use the group-centered approach. There is no doubt that the average group will react against the novel approach the retreat master will assume. Once the novelty of the approach has worn off, the retreatants will actively resist the new responsibility they must assume. The common reaction of many to the leader who will not assume the "normal" role of leadership is great hostility. Though such hostility will often be expressed in an indirect manner, the leader will feel its effects and a great deal of personal security will be required to tolerate the anxieties of the group.

The realistic group-centered leader will necessarily ask himself how much hostility he can absorb in the face of anxiety-producing circumstances. He will also know that groups will often exhibit a lack of progress over long periods of time. Much indecision, frustration, and impatience will be displayed during these unproductive periods. This will undoubtedly be difficult to tolerate. The temptation to return to safe and acceptable behavior will be intense at times. The drive to take charge again and lead the group out of their confusion may often become overwhelming.

It cannot be overemphasized that the extent to which one yields to such temptations will determine how much the potential experience will be destroyed. If one were to take charge and direct the experience, the basic goal of diffusing leadership would obviously not be accomplished. All the other goals implicit in the approach depend upon the retreatants recognizing their own capacity. Removing the responsibility from their shoulders will reduce the chances of their striving for the goal of self-direction.

There is a direct relation between the leader's tolerance of diverse behavior and his faith in the group. When the leader takes it upon himself to alter a certain kind of behavior, he exhibits a lack of trust in the group's capacity to reach its goals in the most effective manner possible. Sensing this lack of trust, the retreatants cannot effectively follow the course which will, in fact, be the most conducive to satisfying group needs.

Next to actually being able to tolerate diverse behavior within the group, the retreat master will be most effective when he realizes his own inadequacy in tolerating hostility or lack of direction within the group. Rather than recognizing the low tolerance level for what it is and accepting it as such, retreat masters often counter hostility with hostility. A far more realistic approach under such conditions would be a verbal expression to the group of the desire to return the hostility. The leader thereby relieves himself of the burden which has become troublesome without disrupting whatever dynamic has been created up to that point. Honest expressions of internal feelings need never be feared. On the contrary, such honesty can often be an example which will demonstrate the value of openness to all.

SUMMARY

If one were to attempt to sum up this chapter, he would have to say that the reason for its inclusion is to emphasize the fact that it is even more difficult for the retreat master than for the participants to grow in the philosophy presented in past chapters. While it is easy to say, for example, that one should trust others and believe in their inherent ability to seek their own good, it is quite difficult to live according to this principle. As long as the principle remains in the abstract realm, a great number would affirm the truth of such a conclusion. But in actually attempting to relate to others and demonstrate this principle of motivating behavior there are but a few willing to endure the frustration, anxiety, and pain such behavior requires.

Because of the difficulty involved in attempting to describe the emotional experience, the present discussion does not begin to point out the seriousness of the dangers and difficulties involved in releasing the dynamics within a group. Only to the extent that a leader is able to take risks in working with a group will he be able to create an atmosphere conducive to bringing persons closer together in their concerns. While one might emphasize the rewards which are immediately connected with such an approach, it would be unrealistic not to suggest the negative side of the experience. Rather than allow individuals to be unaware of the negative aspects, it would be better to have some very capable persons refuse to take the necessary risks.

Even the so-called negative aspects of beginning such an approach do nothing in the end but encourage more personal growth than was previously possible. There is no easy way to facilitate such growth. There are times when the attempt seems worthless and self-defeating. In the long run, however, nothing is more rewarding than taking the risks involved in order to develop oneself and to witness the positive growth in others.

10.   on becoming a christian

"Blessed are the poor in spirit,
for theirs is the kingdom of heaven"

As a result of the retreat experience which has been successful in creating a safe and free atmosphere, one may be acutely aware of retreatants turning away from their own false images of themselves. When the individual is able to take an honest look at himself without the normal fear that he will be rejected for doing so, persons become conscious of their own tendency to hide from others. The retreatant gradually becomes aware of the fact that there is a significant gap between the person he is and that person he projects to others.

When the atmosphere is truly free, the retreatants discover this freedom in a personal way which allows them to consider their own course for the future. They express this freedom in a manner which suggests that they could maintain the facade if they desire, but the fact is that within this desire for independence is a basic drive for self-expression. Along with a sense of shame for having hidden their identity comes an intense desire to allow others an insight into their own true self.

As the retreatants use the retreat to explore the difference between the self they experience and the self they manifest to others, their distaste for continuing to play the false role grows. Maintaining this facade in their day-to-day relationships the retreatants have created many internal conflicts which they feel could be dissolved by being honest with themselves and others. There are times when the false image projects itself beyond the relationship with others and into one's relationship with God.

It suddenly dawns on me! This business of role-playing isn't confined to those I can expect I might reasonably deceive. I don't even *pray* honestly — that is, I don't really speak to God from my heart. Most of the time I'm just saying things I figure I am supposed to be saying. I don't even know where — or, who — where did I get the idea it is better to say some things to God and not others. What a stupid situation! God certainly knows what's in my heart. Why should I try to fool him? . . . Man, I am really in bad shape! I'm not just trying to fool others. I'm trying to fool God.

This student, like many others, got a sudden insight into the depths of his own deceptive existence. Through a sudden inspiration, the basic definition of prayer as a lifting of the heart and mind to God had genuine meaning for the first time. Due to this student's propensity to hide his genuine feelings, he was unable to even relate properly in his prayer life. This tendency to play a role was carried into an area where it could not conceivably make any sense. Such reactions are not uncommon in the retreat which concentrates on freeing individuals to honestly explore themselves and their relationship to God.

Experience indicates that great numbers of people do not have much self-esteem. For any number of possible reasons, they are not pleased with their personal identity and consequently spend a great deal of psychic energy in constructing elaborate defenses which will hide this identity from others. In classical religious terms, this psychological mechanism might be described as the sin of pride. An attempt to conceal weaknesses, whether real or imaginary, specifically describes the sin of pride as defined by most spiritual writers.

In the context of the retreat experience, one may watch individuals becoming aware of this self-pride and slowly dispensing with some of the more obvious facades which protect them from revealing their true identity to others. While such a process is distressing enough, it becomes even more disturbing when these same individuals find themselves removing masks they were not even conscious of wearing. Continuing such a quest is a deeply disturbing experience. Since major surgery is often required to remove a facade which was always considered an integral part of one's personality, it is not surprising to discover individuals encountering painful emotional upheavals in the process. The mysterious fact is, however, that under the influence of personal freedom individuals do move in positive directions despite the pain involved.

To offer a retreatant the opportunity to remove the facades and masks which hide him from others gives him the ability and the opportunity to manifest true poverty of spirit. When an individual takes concrete steps toward manifesting himself openly and honestly before all men, he is certainly minimizing any tendency toward pride and exhibiting the honest humility which would encourage all to accept him. Placed in an atmosphere free of fear and threat, there is no doubt that many find the courage to move positively themselves and aid others to do the same. If it is possible for a retreat experience to offer this practical opportunity for development one would certainly be remiss in denying anyone this experience.

"Blessed are the meek,
for they shall possess the earth"

A type of facade which is gradually removed in the course of the retreat is the perception of what one "ought to be," how he "ought to react," and what kind of goals he "ought to seek." Though often so subtly expressed that even the retreatant is not aware of the dimensions, such perceptions of self are normally rooted deep within the personality structure of the individual. This false image of self with which many are constantly preoccupied is difficult to remove.

When one reflects on the normal developmental situation for children, it is not difficult to see why the false perception of self is so much a part of the personality. So many parents are preoccupied with telling children how they "ought to be," that it is not surprising that many absorb these personality traits at the deepest emotional level. Since they were absorbed at an early age when the emotional content of personality dominated, removing such perceptions is naturally a difficult process.

When retreatants speak of their personal goals, they not uncommonly recognize the irrational control which these "ought to" constructs exercise on their personality. It is evident in their attempt to move out from under such control that a great deal of effort must be exerted to make even some movement toward acceptance of actual emotions and feelings. The struggle to move away from unrealistic expectations is normally difficult and the rewards for making such movement are often limited, but most find the direction fulfilling enough to continue the quest.

As in the discussion of facades, an individual suddenly realizing the meaning of prayer demonstrates the dynamic of this facade. As many form friendship on the basis of acting and reacting according to some irrational demands outside themselves, some discover that even their prayer life is founded on this kind of nonpersonal level. Thus one Sister, describing her discovery of an impersonal relationship through prayer, suggests how such thinking developed.

> I guess it must have started in the novitiate with all those rules and regulations. It was understood that if you really loved God that you would be able to spend long hours in the chapel. Love of God . . . that is, no one could talk to God of love unless it took the form of an endurance contest. And all those formula prayers. It was important to just say prayers whether you meant them or not. It got so I was afraid to engage in mental prayer because it didn't sound like anything that we read. Now I suddenly realize that we are creating a false god by this kind of ritual. If he is interested in words that are not mine and do not spring from within my soul, he cannot be someone I can love. Who can? . . . what kind of love is that?

The dynamics of the spiritual relationship with God closely parallel the same tendencies to grow in personal relationships with others. Interestingly enough, the growth as well as the obstacles to growth are more pronounced in the spiritual relationship. Thus the retreat manifests another aid to spiritual growth insofar as it demonstrates in a practical way the human analogy to spiritual development. By intimately experiencing both the dimensions of human and spiritual maturation, the individual will be able to link the two and use the experience of one to aid development in the other.

We are all familiar with the distorted view of meekness which for one reason or another is common throughout our society. The popular caricature of the meek man is one who withdraws from others as much as possible. When he is forced to engage socially he protects himself by withdrawing as much as possible from any conversation. In all of this stereotype reaction, the meek man epitomizes the diametrically opposite reactions normally associated with genuine humility and charity.

The poor man or meek man in the Old Testament accepted suffering patiently from God's hands. The crucial difference here is that this is not the same as suffering patiently at the mercy of others. One who suffered patiently by accepting God's plan for his life would not hide from his true identity. Especially crucial in the virtue of meekness is the courage to project one's true self to others.

If we are to blame anyone for the self that is distasteful in our own eyes, we must blame God. Whether we are able to accept or reject this identity, it is fashioned by the divine and part of our inheritance. To say that I "ought to" feel a certain way rather than the way "I do feel" is another attempt to say that I will not accept the self offered to me by God. The truly meek man does not withdraw from others; but rather stands honestly before them by projecting himself in what he considers both his strength and weakness. It takes a great deal of courage to become a meek person who accepts suffering patiently from God's hands. But the person who makes this courageous move toward discovering one's self discovers the real meaning in life which will allow him to "possess the earth."

> *"Blessed are they who mourn,*
> *for they shall be comforted"*

It becomes increasingly difficult to escape the pressures to conform in modern society. The necessity to accept the standards of the establishment in order to "move ahead" in the company oppresses the individual. Many find self-expression a barrier to progress and conformity the easiest path to success. We increasingly accept the basic tenets of adapting ourselves to the will of the majority in even the most personal aspects of our life.

If those outside the industrial complex do not consume the fruits of labor, we are warned that our "standard of living" will be endangered. Advertising agencies attempt to discover and even create needs within the average person which will motivate him to consume as much as possible. There is an increasing tendency to sell products to persons in order to satisfy their desire to "be one of the crowd." Because the societal pressures to conform are increasing it is not difficult to see the individual becoming a victim of his environment.

Recent studies in the area of education indicate that one of the most significant results of a "good" education is the increased conformity on the part of the student. Evidently the student discovers early in his career that it is easier to digest the views and opinions of his professors than it is to take the effort to argue effectively from another point of view. The degree appears to have become increasingly thought of in terms of a ticket into the business world. It is as if the university knew the need for conformity was necessary in the business world and, therefore, subtly rewarded behavior which would best qualify the student for his later life.

Finally, we find the path of conformity being traveled with greater frequency in religion. Though recent years have revealed more and more individuals desperately searching for meaning in their faith, far too many think of religion in terms of rules and ritual. This appears to be just one more manifestation of the desire to be part of the group without exerting any distinctive individuality.

With the expectations of society forming a continuum with the goals instilled early by parents, it is not surprising that few are able to counter the tendency to live according to external norms. The expectations of others are so much a part of our entire life that we are frequently unaware of the fact that most of our life is governed by these external rules. Once one has reflected honestly on this situation for a period of time, however, there is a tendency to reject such guidelines in favor of internal goals.

When a person is able to look at this tendency reflectively, he begins to see that a certain frustration is implicit in patterned conformity. In order to conform to the expectation of others, one must have some ability to predict the words, thoughts, and actions toward which others will react positively. A constant dilemma faces us in trying to predict what is expected of us in any given situation or set of circumstances. The result is a constant state of anxiety and self-consciousness concerning our personal responses to others.

Possibly the most destructive thing about constantly meeting the expectations of others is that we are rarely able to enter into anything honestly. Our work becomes mechanical and meaningless because it is not an expression of ourselves. Under such circumstances, our creativity is severely limited if not extinguished. Whether it involves meeting new people or organizing large numbers, our lack of personal involvement can severely limit creative expression as well as personal growth.

As a result of the retreat experience, persons are apparently more willing to take the risks necessary to express themselves openly and honestly before others. They still labor under the pressure to conform, but there is more willingness to discover personal goals which are unrelated to external expectations. The meaning of self-expression suddenly becomes more vitally important to personal growth whether others approve or disapprove.

The retreatants have discovered the fulfillment in self-expression, but they have also become aware of fear and anxiety which must be endured in moving toward that goal. A great deal of internal conflict is a normal part of moving away from external expectations and into self to discover meaning. Despite the realization through experience of the suffering involved in personal fulfillment, the retreatants generally desire to move in that direction as swiftly as possible. Enduring internal conflict appears to be a small price to pay for the reward of self-expression.

*"Blessed are they who hunger and thirst for justice,
for they shall be satisfied"*

The Old Testament concept of justice to which Jesus was undoubtedly referring is that moral and religious perfection which results from perfect fidelity to God's will. In the Old Testament context, the God of wrath made heavy demands upon man and insisted upon a strict accounting. To deviate even momentarily from strict fidelity could bring judgment swiftly and definitively. It becomes obvious in the light of the New Testament, however, that the sanctions are external to the fidelity which becomes the essence of justice.

In the time of Christ, the established Church had become fascinated with the sanctions imposed upon those who deviated from external observance. The law had become minutely expressed in terms of its demands and its sanctions. The scribes and Pharisees were so preoccupied with the letter of the law that they had nearly snuffed out the spirit which gives it life. The burden upon individuals had become nearly intolerable.

One of the most significant aspects of Christ's mission was his teaching regarding this necessary fidelity to the will of God. In contrast to the unconditional acceptance which Christ manifested to the sinner, he was severe in his criticism of the doctors of the Church. In order to reach the goal of fidelity to God's will most perfectly, man must be stimulated by love rather than coerced by sanctions. The goal remains constant, but Christ insists on a more powerful means to that end. While justice is the constant goal toward which all men must strive, the pharisaical notion of a legal justice must be purified in order for men to understand its nature and, therefore, strive for it in the most perfect manner.

In the Church today, we still have men clinging to a distorted notion of a legalized religion. In their effort to quantify obligations, they have lost the sense of spontaneous love which will allow them to most perfectly recognize and accept God's will in their lives. If they become preoccupied with the legal requirements of their religion, they will easily abstract themselves from the inner promptings of their hearts which speak of more serious obligations imposed upon them as followers of Christ. One is certainly more secure if he is preoccupied with the rite and ritual of religion rather than being concerned over the suffering of fellow human beings.

As a result of the retreat experience, many turn within themselves to discover the meaning and direction of their lives. Rather than looking for the acceptance of others through external means, they become more identified with an expression of themselves. They become more consciously aware of the fact that conformity to external criteria alone will not create the Christian mentality toward which they are drawn. In many ways, one might say that they move from an Old Testament concept of justice to the purified notion as expressed by Christ.

As with so many of the facades previously described group members slowly discover themselves living in a world created by demands outside of themselves. From early childhood, they feel they have led their lives according to the dictates of others. In their drive to please others, they suddenly find themselves on a stage before the entire world living a life regulated by external expectations. In the process of satisfying others, they have distorted even their own identity.

With the freedom to reflect seriously on the direction they have allowed others to give to their lives, many find a sincere desire to express their identity to others. Though they know such a path will leave them open to rejection by those around them, the desire to live their lives in a manner which more perfectly expresses their own strengths and weaknesses will not be denied. Rather than habitually doing the things which will please others they are willing to move in directions which will express convictions which lie deep within themselves.

The fear that one is basically evil keeps most men from ever looking within themselves, let alone expressing genuine feelings. Because of impressions which have resulted from experience in one's particular cultural or family norms, man has accepted without question the belief that his own genuine feelings cannot be trusted. After an experience which permits one the freedom to explore such feelings honestly at a level which reveals these feelings in their totality one discovers he need not fear such emotion. Though some emotions give one cause for concern, none of them need be feared and most will be accepted as neither good nor bad but rather as part of oneself. With an ability to explore these emotions without fear, there is the potential to discover the emotion of love. One begins to understand Christ's words which placed so much emphasis on love. A rich experience of love upon which to build will help make clear why Christ made this the central point of his message to men. The force, power, and beauty of love become realities, rather than abstractions. One knows how to hunger and thirst after justice because he has experienced the means at a much deeper level than ever before.

> *"Blessed are the merciful,*
> *for they shall obtain mercy"*

This beatitude turns on a New Testament term for "merciful" which not only implies compassion but an effective remedy for distress. There is a very subtle but real distinction between our concept of mercy which strongly accents compassion and the term Christ uses which balances this compassion with an action that alleviates the distress of those in need of money. The first concept suggests a judge making his decision compassionately and with sympathy for the sufferings of the accused. In the context of the latter example one can see that mercy which actively involves one person with another in a way which can relieve much of the anxiety in the accused.

All of us are in desperate need of the kind of mercy Christ suggests we share with one another. We experience frustrations, setbacks, and failures in our daily lives which leave us in need of the active compassion which will alleviate the anxiety created as a result of vicissitudes. We all at times search for reassurance from others during the course of our lives.

As much as we seek this opportunity to share our suffering with others rarely do we open ourselves to the possibility. It seems that such suffering creates more isolation rather than an occasion for communication and growth. Because of an undefined fear which prevents us from revealing our weakness to others, we build a wall around ourselves and thereby prevent others from giving or receiving mercy. This vicious circle can become a source of such isolation that we become less and less aware of the part that all men suffer and are capable of sharing this grief with one another.

After a certain period in the context of the retreat, however, many find the courage and strength necessary to reveal some of their own anxiety. They will hesitantly suggest the courses which have prevented them from overcoming periods of depression, for example. If the statement is projected with honesty and sincerity, others will naturally accept it. Either because they share some of the same feeling or because they naturally respond with compassion toward one in need of mercy, the group begins to make an effort to ease the distress of a fellow member.

As more and more group members begin to use the occasion to share their concerns with others, there is greater opportunity within the retreat experience to understand the basic meaning of mercy. This kind of genuine interaction which suggests active concern necessarily implies a passivity as well as an activity. When one genuinely projects understanding toward another, he will come to realize that such a movement will normally imply a reciprocation.

For whatever reasons one might suggest, there is an isolation from others predominant in our society. As a result of this isolation, it is not uncommon for individuals to feel that their own reactions to themselves are somehow unique. As one speaks honestly about his personal reactions to himself, his religious convictions or about others who surround him, he normally incites some kind of common reaction within the group. What often appears as a fear of rejection from others turns out to be a reaction dominant in the group assembled. At times it is possible to sense the group's relief when someone has had the courage to suggest the very thing which was in the hearts of each member.

The relief such a confession offers to the group assembled cannot be measured adequately. Many have expended a great deal of psychic energy attempting to hide their desire to be the kind of person others might reject. When they suddenly realize there is no need to continue this facade, they are free to accept both themselves and others in this particular human weakness. The compassion they feel extends simultaneously to themselves and others. They truly obtain mercy because they are merciful.

> *"Blessed are the clean of heart,*
> *for they shall see God"*

In attempting to clarify the meaning of the phrase "clean of heart," it might be appropriate to reflect on the prophets' fight for justice. In the midst of their difficult struggle, they always maintain a clean and clear purity of intention. The temptation to minimize their message for the sake of those to whom they preached must have been intense at times, but they never lost sight of that purity of language which projected their message in the clearest manner possible.

The meaning of the biblical phrase "clean of heart" might be best described as sincerity. The clean of heart convey to themselves and others genuine and honest reactions which spring directly from the heart. The spontaneity of their speech and manner displays an earnest attempt to discover the most basic truths about themselves and others regardless of the risks involved.

Progress toward this kind of sincerity can be witnessed when a person is deeply involved in the free and spontaneous atmosphere of the retreat. In the early stages of progress, the individual identifies the movement in a personal manner. Many retreatants describe the new experience as a kind of peace with themselves. In contrast to past efforts which were designed to block out certain kinds of awareness of personal experience, they now speak of comfort and even joy in recognizing and living with knowledge they would have previously attempted to suppress.

Because of the emphasis given to the serenity one ultimately feels in living with his emotions, some might think of the process as occurring easily. The truth is that the movement in positive directions can occur only with the greatest difficulty. From common experience, one can readily understand the personal rejection of certain aspects of his personality. Every man has emotional characteristics which he has rejected and can only tentatively accept as part of himself. It is reasonable to expect that because suppression has been part of his personality structure for so many years, one will not be able to reverse the trend suddenly without suffering a great deal of anxiety in the process.

When the climate is such that his first tentative steps are reinforced by acceptance and understanding of those who surround him, the individual is able to move more honestly towards himself and his feelings. He realizes that others will not automatically reject him for genuine feelings which he himself has attempted to repress, and is then able to explore those negative feelings and emotions with more honesty and sincerity. It is under these circumstances that the individual begins to discover the comfort in accepting and even embracing emotions which previously caused him nothing but anxiety.

As the person begins to discover his personal experience is an asset rather than some frightening and destructive tendency, this comfort, with his feelings, grows to become a fascination. He will be inclined to stop at times and consider his feelings in an effort to come closer to himself. Watching a person patiently consider the exact shading of a particular emotion gives one the sense that the individual is listening to signals emanating from deep within himself. The fear that was once preventing this kind of discovery has neither been stamped out nor extinguished, but rather gradually dissolves as a result of the genuine desire to move toward self-actualization.

It appears that only from this vantage point of acceptance of self will we be able to understand sincerity in its most fundamental sense. For persons close to their own reactions and emotions, the problem of pursuing the most honest course in life becomes less and less difficult. From this superior awareness of themselves, such persons not only basically realize the honest course of action but have difficulty in moving in any other direction.

There is little doubt that the clean of heart do see God. The special blessing which comes to the sincere individual who is courageous enough to take the risks involved in being honest with himself are obvious to all who are willing to witness such blessings. As one begins to appreciate himself in his complexity, he also grows in a greater awareness of his reactions, desires, frustrations, and the general emotional impact, of his existence. With such awareness, comes a greater and greater ability to appreciate life with a renewed sense of awe and wonder.

> *"Blessed are the peacemakers,*
> *for they shall be called the children of God"*

Anyone who has reflected honestly on the gospel story cannot help but be impressed by the theme of peace which permeates the text both implicitly and explicitly. In sharp contrast to the Old Testament, the New Testament conveys a word of peace. It is as if Christ were coming not just to speak of peace, but actually to generate it by his presence. From the time of Christ's birth until his return after his death, he appeared to be adamant in his desire to bring peace to the hearts of men.

In moving toward his goal, however, Christ met with difficulties. As his preaching continued, more and more were disturbed by what he said. People became increasingly hostile to the message he was proclaiming. It became obvious to all, including Christ, that only through his death would this hostility be put to an end. Despite all external threats, however, he remained intent on bringing peace wherever he went.

Through loving acceptance, Christ spread a message of peace to all whom he encountered. Because he was able to accept individuals as they were — crippled, blind, mute and sinful — they were better able to accept themselves. By personifying the peace he hoped to generate, Christ was able to instruct others in this virtue which he felt was so important.

As one becomes more and more sensitive to the needs of others, he tends toward an acceptance which implies neither judgment nor sympathy. In sincerely attempting to understand another human being in his unique existence, the accepting person receives the other as he is. Without being either exceedingly pleased by the individual's virtues or repelled by his vices, the person generating acceptance simply moves to understand the mystery of the person before him.

When encountered by such an attitude, even the hostile and belligerent are most likely to reflect upon their own actions. When others are willing to accept one as he is, there is reason for him to wonder if it would not be possible for him to accept himself. In further considering such a unique attitude, the person displaying hostility gradually develops the courage necessary to abandon his defenses, at least temporarily, and to see himself as others see him. Even the aggressively hostile functioning with this attitude tends to move towards a state of equilibrium and peace.

More than easing the tensions for the aggressive person, however, the atmosphere of acceptance generates a sense of peace which few have been able to experience in their lives. When individuals are able to manifest acceptance toward one another through their exchange of ideas, feelings and emotions, a great calm develops within the group. Since there is no longer the necessity to spend a great deal of effort in maintaining elaborate defenses against attack from others, people are able to relax and view both themselves and others with a tranquility they have never known before.

Even in an atmosphere of acceptance which many groups are able to generate, however, there will always remain some aggressiveness toward one another. Whether such feelings are intentional or not, some of the pain appears to be relieved when the hostility has been released. As the experience proceeds, the hard, insensitive, and inflexible person becomes more aware of himself and his effect upon others. With such awareness, he gradually tempers his impact on others due to the new reflectivity he has been able to adopt.

In evaluating personal feelings, it is easy to see why judgment of one by another would be extremely threatening. This is particularly true when such judgments imply pressure from another to change a personal attitude, emotion, or approach to life. When such threats are perceived directly, defenses are automatically devised in order to defend one's self-image. Such judgments, are diametrically opposed to the principles of group dynamics outlined thus far. In order to gain that internal peace necessary to help others, an atmosphere of acceptance is required which is the result of the nonjudgmental understanding of at least one other person.

Peace will only come at a price. Only through conquering the most serious threats to one's internal perceptions of himself will one be able to bring about an atmosphere conducive to peace of heart. To achieve an ability to share in Christ's role as peacemaker will be reward enough for those earnestly striving to live the beatitudes.

> *"Blessed are they who suffer persecution*
> *for Justice' sake, for theirs is the kingdom of heaven"*

As has been suggested earlier, societal and parental demands in our life predispose most persons to yield to the demands of others. We are conditioned from the earliest years not only to yield to the advice of others but also to give advice constantly. With the constant barrage of advice, instruction, and demands pressing us in so many different directions simultaneously, it is almost impossible to move without incurring judgment upon our actions from others. It is not uncommon, therefore, to find individuals in a constant state of tension concerning their life projects.

Since they are so concerned over the conflict between themselves and the demands placed on them by others, many do not ever seriously consider their own desires and goals. The last thing that would occur to many would be to trust their own innate tendencies. Probably because moving on their own initiative would mean bearing more responsibility for their actions than they feel capable of assuming, individuals normally look beyond themselves for the direction of their lives. Consequently, barriers are erected to keep us from reaching the goal of self-actualization.

Without the courage to move in directions dictated by internal drives, individuals eliminate the most effective means to creativity. Carl Rogers surely had this in mind when he wrote in his essay, "To Be That Self Which One Truly Is":

> Watching my clients, I have come to a much better understanding of creative people. El Greco, for example, must have realized as he looked at some of his early work, that "good artists do not paint like that." But somehow he trusted his own experiencing of life, the process of himself, sufficiently that he could go on expressing his own unique perceptions. It was as though he could say, "Good artists do not paint like this, but I paint like this." Or to move to another field, Ernest Hemingway was surely aware that "good writers do not write like this." But fortunately he moved toward being Hemingway, being himself, rather than toward someone else's conception of a good writer. Einstein seems to have been unusually oblivious to the fact that good physicists did not think this kind of thoughts. Rather than drawing back because of his inadequate academic preparation in physics, he simply moved toward being Einstein, toward thinking his own thoughts, toward being as truly and deeply himself as he could. This is not a phenomenon which occurs only in the artist or the genius. Time and again in my clients, I have seen simple people become significant and creative in their own sphere, as they have developed more trust of the processes going on within themselves, and have dared to feel their own feelings,

live by values which they discover within, and express themselves in their own unique ways.

As a result of the retreat experience, many people have been able to move in a direction which would indicate that they are better able to trust their own inherent drive toward self-fulfillment. Though such development begins with a significant degree of hesitation, there is greater and greater growth as the satisfaction implicit in such self-trust increases. As with the significant persons mentioned by Rogers, each individual realizes his own unique importance and consequently gains esteem in his own eyes and the eyes of others.

Parallel with this personal development, persons also tend to gain a new and penetrating concept of their relationship to God. They are no longer satisfied with a ritualistic approach to religion. It is no longer sufficient for others to say that this is the manner in which one "ought" to relate to God. The important question is now, "How do I as a unique individual best relate to God?" Far from abandoning religious practice, individuals with fresh insights begin to look for meaning in religious practice and thereby attain a greater personal involvement in the experience of religion.

As the creative relate to their particular art form, it is also important for truly religious persons to be creative in their attempts to relate genuinely to God. It is no longer sufficient to adopt a passive attitude toward religion. Observing some so-called religious individuals, one gets the impression that they expect instant salvation simply because they have performed predetermined rites. Such a superstitious and magical approach to religion is not sufficient for anyone who has begun to discover the meaning and value of himself in relation to God.

"Blessed are you when men reproach you, and persecute you, and, speaking falsely, say all manner of evil against you, for my sake. Rejoice and exult, for so did they persecute the prophets who were before you."

The approach to retreats suggested here is more than a new technique or format. To add a group discussion in order to fulfill the demands necessitated by a new element of thinking in the Church is to miss the point altogether. The idea of introducing the dynamic into retreats introduces an entirely new attitude toward man's relationship with God. The successful retreat of the future must necessarily approach men with this attitude in order to be successful, whether group discussion is a part of the retreat or not.

The basic idea in introducing the discussion is to give retreatants a chance to practice the virtues of Christian love while they discuss them. Rather than trying to instill an intellectual appreciation for religion in hopes that some of this will result in future conviction, the dynamic would ask people to consider whether or not they are prepared to practice Christianity. To allow individuals to reject this possibility is not only fundamental to the retreat dynamic; but basic to Christianity itself.

The strong feeling which prevails concerning the group dynamics retreat is that it introduces an entirely new element into the experience. If one were to attempt to isolate the element, he would have to say that it is the dimension of community. From this new dimension, many have experienced more profoundly the results traditionally expected to occur in the retreat. Personal experience has led a great number of people to conclude that such a result was not accidental. When individuals speculate further on this point, they normally conclude that the genuine meaning of community is only vaguely realized and insufficiently explored in the world today. The sincere hope is that the retreat dynamic will be a positive move toward discovering much of the power and goodness implicit in the meaning of community life.